Choose Joy

Choose Joy

3-MINUTE DEVOTIONS
FOR WOMEN

BARBOUR BOOKS
An Imprint of Barbour Publishing, Inc.

© 2017 by Barbour Publishing, Inc.

Print ISBN: 978-1-63409-998-1

Readings are compiled and have been adapted from *Daily Wisdom for Women 2013 Collection, Daily Wisdom for Women 2014 Collection, Everyday Joy, Everyday Encouragement, Everyday Hope*, and *365 Encouraging Verses of the Bible*. Published by Barbour Publishing, Inc. All rights reserved.

Our mission is to publish and distribute inspirational products offering exceptional value and biblical encouragement to the masses.

Member of the
Evangelical Christian
Publishers Association

Printed in the United States of America.

Introduction

*I'm thanking you, God, from a full heart, I'm writing
the book on your wonders. I'm whistling, laughing, and
jumping for joy; I'm singing your song, High God.*

PSALM 9:1–2 MSG

These devotions are especially for those days when you need
a bit of encouragement and a gentle reminder to: CHOOSE
JOY! Three minutes from your busy day is all you'll need to
refresh your spirit and fill your cup to overflowing with joy
for the journey.

- ❀ MINUTE 1: *Read and reflect on God's Word.*

- ❀ MINUTE 2: *Read the devotion and think about
    how it applies to your life.*

- ❀ MINUTE 3: *Pray.*

Although these devotions aren't meant as a tool for deep
Bible study, they can be a touchstone to keep you grounded
and focused on God, the giver of joy. May this book remind
you that delight can be discovered in the everyday moments
of life.

Joy in the Morning

*All who seek the L*ORD *will praise him.*
Their hearts will rejoice with everlasting joy.
PSALM 22:26 NLT

Every day, God provides us with beauty all around to cheer
and help us. It may come through the beauty of flowers or
the bright blue sky—or maybe the white snow covering the
trees of a glorious winter wonderland. It may be through the
smile of a child or the grateful face of the one we care for.
Each and every day, the Lord has a special gift to remind us
of whose we are and to generate the joy we need to succeed.

Lord God, I thank You for Your joy; I thank You for
providing it every day to sustain me. I will be joyful in You.

He Enjoys You

The LORD your God is in your midst, a mighty one who will save; he will rejoice over you with gladness; he will quiet you by his love; he will exult over you with loud singing.

ZEPHANIAH 3:17 ESV

Zephaniah's words remind us that God is our loving parent. Our mighty Savior offers us a personal relationship, loving and rejoicing over us, His children, glad that we live and move in Him. He is the Lord of the universe, and yet He will quiet our restless hearts and minds with His tender love. He delights in our lives and celebrates our union with Him. We can rest in His affirmation and love no matter what circumstances surround us.

Lord, help me remember that You are always with me and that You delight in me. Remind me that I am Your child and that You enjoy our relationship.

Sweet Aroma

The heartfelt counsel of a friend is as
sweet as perfume and incense.
PROVERBS 27:9 NLT

Whether it's over coffee, over dessert, or even on the phone, a cherished friend can offer the encouragement and God-directed counsel we all need from time to time. Friendships that have Christ as their center are wonderful relationships blessed by the Father. Through the timely, godly advice these friends offer, God speaks to us, showering us with comfort that is as sweet as perfume and incense. So what are you waiting for? Make a date with a friend and share the sweet aroma of Jesus!

Jesus, Your friendship means the world to me. I value
the close friendships You've blessed me with, too! Thank You
for the special women in my life. Show me every day how
to be a blessing to them just as they are to me.

The New Me

Therefore, if anyone is in Christ,
the new creation has come:
The old has gone, the new is here!
2 CORINTHIANS 5:17 NIV

Are you in Christ? Is He consistently Lord of your life? Then you are a new creation. *Everything* is new. What's history is done and over—and Jesus has replaced your old with His new: new peace, new joy, new love, new strength. Since God Himself sees us as a new creation, how can we do any less? We need to choose to see ourselves as a new creation, too. And we can, through God's grace. Be glad. Give thanks. Live each day as the new creation you have become through Jesus.

Father, I'm so thankful that You are a God of grace—
and I thank You that I am a new creation. Please give
me the spiritual eyes to see myself as a new creation,
looking past the guilt of yesterday's choices.

Unchained!

The Spirit you received does not make you slaves,
so that you live in fear again, rather, the Spirit you received
brought about your adoption to sonship.
And by him we cry, "Abba, Father."

ROMANS 8:15 NIV

Do you struggle with fear? Do you feel it binding you with its invisible chains? If so, then there's good news. Through Jesus, you have received the Spirit of sonship. A son (or daughter) of the Most High God has nothing to fear. Knowing you've been set free is enough to make you cry, "Abba, Father!" in praise. Today, acknowledge your fears to the Lord. He will loose your chains and set you free.

Lord, thank You that You are the great chain-breaker!
I don't have to live in fear. I am Your child,
Your daughter, and You are my Daddy-God!

People Pleaser vs. God Pleaser

*We are not trying to please people
but God, who tests our hearts.*

1 THESSALONIANS 2:4 NIV

When we allow ourselves to be real before God, it doesn't matter what others think. If the God of the universe has accepted us, then who cares about someone else's opinion? It is impossible to please both God and man. We must make a choice. Man looks at the outward appearance, but God looks at the heart. Align your heart with His. Let go of impression management, which focuses on outward appearance. Receive God's unconditional love and enjoy the freedom to be yourself before Him!

Dear Lord, may I live for You alone. Help me transition from a people pleaser to a God pleaser. Amen.

He Will Send Help

The waves of death swirled about me; the torrents
of destruction overwhelmed me.... In my distress
I called to the LORD.... From his temple he
heard my voice; my cry came to his ears.

2 SAMUEL 22:5, 7 NIV

God never asked us to do life alone. When the waves of death swirl around us and the pounding rain of destruction threatens to overwhelm us, we can cry out to our heavenly Father, knowing that He will not let us drown. He will hear our voice, and He will send help. So next time you feel that you can't put one foot in front of the other, ask God to send you His strength and energy. He will help you to live out your purpose in this chaotic world.

Lord, thank You for strengthening me when the "dailyness"
of life and its various trials threaten to overwhelm me.

Shake It Up!

The LORD had said to Abram, "Leave your native country, your relatives, and your father's family, and go to the land that I will show you. . . . I will bless you. . . and you will be a blessing to others."

GENESIS 12:1-2 NLT

In God's wisdom, He likes to shake us up a little, stretch us out of our comfort zone, push us out on a limb. Yet we resist the change, cling to what's known, and try to change His mind with fat, sloppy tears. Are you facing a big change? God wants you to be willing to embrace change that He brings into your life. Even unbidden change. You may feel as if you're out on a limb, but don't forget that God is the tree trunk. He's not going to let you fall.

Holy, loving Father, in every area of my life teach me to trust You more deeply. Amen.

Release the Music Within

*Those who are wise will find a time
and a way to do what is right.*

ECCLESIASTES 8:5 NLT

It has been said that many people go to their graves with their music still in them. Do you carry a song within your heart that is waiting to be heard?

Whether we are eight or eighty, it is never too late to surrender our hopes and dreams to God. A wise woman trusts that God will help her find the time and manner in which to use her talents for His glory as she seeks His direction. Let the music begin.

Dear Lord, my music is fading against the constant beat of a busy pace. I surrender my gifts to You and pray for the time and manner in which I can use those gifts to touch my world. Amen.

Simply Silly

*A cheerful disposition is
good for your health.*
PROVERBS 17:22 MSG

Imagine the effect we could have on our world today if our countenance reflected the joy of the Lord all of the time: at work, at home, at play. Jesus said, "I have told you this so that my joy may be in you and that your joy may be complete" (John 15:11 NIV). Is your cup of joy full? Have you laughed today? Not a small smile, but laughter. Maybe it's time we looked for something to laugh about and tasted joy. Jesus suggested it.

*Lord, help me find joy this day. Let me laugh
and give praises to the King. Amen.*

Anxious Anticipations

I am not saying this because I am
in need, for I have learned to be content
whatever the circumstances.

PHILIPPIANS 4:11 NIV

Have you ever been so eager for the future that you forgot to be thankful for the present day?

Humans have a tendency to complain about the problems and irritations of life. It's much less natural to appreciate the good things we have—until they're gone. While it's fine to look forward to the future, let's remember to reflect on all of today's blessings—the large and the small—and appreciate all that we *do* have.

Thank You, Lord, for the beauty of today.
Please remind me when I become preoccupied
with the future and forget to enjoy the present.

Refreshing Gift

For we have great joy and consolation in
your love, because the hearts of the saints
have been refreshed by you, brother.

PHILEMON 1:7 NKJV

Jesus always took time for those who reached out to Him. In a crowd of people, He stopped to help a woman who touched Him. His quiet love extended to everyone who asked, whether verbally or with unspoken need. God brings people into our path who need our encouragement. We must consider those around us. Smile and thank the waitress, the cashier, the people who help in small ways. Cheering others can have the effect of an energizing drink of water, allowing them to finish the race with a smile.

Jesus, thank You for being an example of how to
encourage and refresh others. Help me to see their
needs and be willing to reach out. Amen.

Infinite and Personal

Am I a God at hand, saith the LORD,
and not a God afar off?...
Do not I fill heaven and earth?
JEREMIAH 23:23-24 KJV

God says that He is both close at hand and over all there is. Whether your day is crumbling around you or is the best day you have ever had, do you see God in it? Even if the "sky is falling," do you still recognize the One who orders all the planets and all your days? Whether we see Him or not, God tells us He is there. And He's here, too—in the good times and the bad.

Lord, empower me to trust You when it's hard to
remember that You are near. And help me to live
thankfully when times are good. Amen.

Chosen

Before I formed you in the womb I knew [and] approved of you [as My chosen instrument], and before you were born I separated and set you apart, consecrating you.

JEREMIAH 1:5 AMPC

God said that before He formed Jeremiah in his mother's womb, He knew him. God separated him from everyone else to perform a specific task, and He consecrated him for that purpose. We can be sure that if God did that for Jeremiah, He did it for each one of us. Nothing about us or our circumstances surprises God. He knew about everything before we were born. And He ordained that we should walk in those ways because we are uniquely qualified by Him to do so. What an awesome God we serve!

Father, the thought that You chose me before the foundation of the world and set me apart for a specific calling is humbling. You are so good. May I go forward with a renewed purpose in life.

God in the Details

*When we heard of it, our hearts melted and everyone's
courage failed because of you, for the LORD your God
is God in heaven above and on the earth below.*

JOSHUA 2:11 NIV

Sometimes when our lives seem to be under siege from
the demands of work, bills, family, whatever—finding the
work of God amid the strife can be difficult. Even though we
acknowledge His power, we may overlook the gentle touches,
the small ways in which He makes every day a little easier.
Just as the Lord cares for the tiniest bird (Matthew 10:29–31),
so He seeks to be a part of every detail in your life. Look for
Him there.

*Father God, I know You are by my side every day, good or
bad, and that You love and care for me. Help me to see Your
work in my life and in the lives of my friends and family.*

Practicality vs. Passion

Leaving her water jar, the woman went back to the town and said to the people, "Come, see a man who told me everything I ever did. Could this be the Messiah?"

JOHN 4:28-29 NIV

Practicality gave way to passion the day the woman at the well abandoned her task, lay down her jar, and ran into town. Everything changed the day she met a man at the well and He asked her for a drink of water. Although they had never met before, He told her everything she had ever done and then He offered her living water that would never run dry. Do you live with such passion, or do you cling to your water jar? Has an encounter with Christ made an impact that cannot be denied in your life?

Lord, help me to lay down anything that stifles my passion for sharing the good news with others. Amen.

Marvelous Plans

*LORD, you are my God; I will exalt you and praise your
name, for in perfect faithfulness you have done
wonderful things, things planned long ago.*

ISAIAH 25:1 NIV

God has a "promised land" for us all—a marvelous plan for our
lives. Recount and record His faithfulness in your life in the
past, because God has already demonstrated His marvelous
plans to you in so many ways. Then prayerfully anticipate the
future journey with Him. Keep a record of God's marvelous
plans in a journal as He unfolds them day by day. You will
find God to be faithful in the smallest aspects of your life and
oh so worthy of your trust.

---

*Oh Lord, help me to recount Your faithfulness, record Your
faithfulness, and trust Your faithfulness in the future.
For You are my God, and You have done marvelous
things, planned long ago. Amen.*

Life Preservers

My comfort in my suffering is this:
your promise preserves my life.

PSALM 119:50 NIV

In the difficulties of life, God is our life preserver. When we are battered by the waves of trouble, we can expect God to understand and to comfort us in our distress. His Word, like a buoyant life preserver, holds us up in the bad times. But the life preserver only works if you put it on *before* your boat sinks. God will surround you with His love and protection—even if you're unconscious of His presence. He promises to keep our heads above water in the storms of life.

Preserving God, I cling to You as my life preserver.
Keep my head above the turbulent water of caregiving
so I don't drown. Bring me safely to the shore.

A Shadow of the Past

Only Rahab the prostitute and all who are with her in her house shall be spared, because she hid the spies we sent.

JOSHUA 6:17 NIV

Rahab wasn't trapped by her past. It didn't hold her back. She was used by God. Her name has come down to us centuries later because of her bold faith. We all have to deal with a past. But God is able to bring good from a painful past. By the grace and power of God we can make choices in the present that can affect our future. There is transforming power with God. We have hope—no matter what lies behind us.

Holy Spirit, You are always at work. Don't ever stop! Show me a new way, Lord. Help me to make healthier choices for myself and my family. Thank You for Your renewing presence in my life.

Charm Bracelet

But the fruit of the Spirit is love, joy, peace, patience,
kindness, goodness, faithfulness, gentleness,
self-control; against such things there is no law.

GALATIANS 5:22–23 NASB

A charm bracelet is a beautiful way to commemorate milestones or special events. Consider your spiritual charm bracelet. If you had a charm to represent your growth in each of the traits from Galatians 5, how many would you feel comfortable attaching to your bracelet in representation of that achievement? Ask your Father which areas in your Christian walk need the most growth. Do you need to develop those traits more strongly before you would feel comfortable donning your bracelet?

Lord, please show me which milestones of Christian living
I need to focus on in order to have the full markings of the
Holy Spirit in my life. Please help me to grow into
the Christian woman You call me to be. Amen.

Board God's Boat

Then, because so many people were coming and going that they did not even have a chance to eat, he said to them, "Come with me by yourselves to a quiet place and get some rest."

MARK 6:31-32 NIV

The apostles ministered tirelessly—so much so that they had little time to eat. The Lord noticed that they had neglected to take time for themselves. Sensitive to their needs, the Savior instructed them to retreat by boat with Him to a solitary place of rest where He was able to minister to them. Often we allow the hectic pace of daily life to drain us physically and spiritually, and in the process, we deny ourselves time alone to pray and read God's Word. Meanwhile, God patiently waits. So perhaps it's time to board God's boat to a quieter place!

Heavenly Father, in my hectic life I've neglected time apart with You. Help me to board Your boat and stay afloat through spending time in Your Word and in prayer. Amen.

A Child in Need

"For all those things My hand has made, and all those things exist," says the LORD. "But on this one will I look: on him who is poor and of a contrite spirit, and who trembles at My word."

ISAIAH 66:2 NKJV

A humble child of God with a need catches His eye. Though He is always watching over all of us, He is drawn to a child who needs Him. We may need forgiveness, wisdom, courage, endurance, patience, health, protection, or even love. God promises to come to our aid when He sees us with a hand up, reaching for His assistance. What needs do you have in your life today? Raise your hand in prayer to God. He'll take care of your needs and then some—blessing your life in ways you can't even imagine!

Father, thank You for caring about the needs of Your children. Help me to remember to always seek You first.

The Secret of Serendipity

A happy heart makes the face cheerful.

PROVERBS 15:13 NIV

Can you remember the last time you laughed in wild abandon? Better yet, when was the last time you did something fun, outrageous, or out of the ordinary? Perhaps it was an activity you haven't done since you were a child, like slip down a waterslide, strap on a pair of ice skates, or pitch a tent and camp overnight. A happy heart turns life's situations into opportunities for fun. When we seek innocent pleasures, we glean the benefits of a happy heart. So try a bit of whimsy just for fun. And rediscover the secret of serendipity.

Dear Lord, because of You, I have a happy heart.
Lead me to do something fun and
spontaneous today! Amen.

A Very Important Phrase

And it came to pass...

FOUND MORE THAN 400 TIMES IN THE KING JAMES BIBLE

There are times in life when we think we can't bear one more day, one more hour, one more minute. But no matter how bad things seem at the time, they are temporary. What's really important is how we handle the opportunities before us today, whether we let our trials defeat us or we look for the hand of God in everything. Every day, week, and year are made up of things that "come to pass"—so even if we fail, we needn't be disheartened. Other opportunities—better days—will come. Let's look past those hard things today and glorify the name of the Lord.

Lord Jesus, how awesome it is that You send or allow these little things that will come to pass. May we recognize Your hand in them today and praise You for them.

The White Knight

Then I will rejoice in the LORD.
I will be glad because he rescues me.

PSALM 35:9 NLT

We're all waiting for someone to rescue us. We wait and wait and wait. . . The truth is, God doesn't want you to exist in a perpetual state of waiting. Live your life—your whole life—by seeking daily joy in the Savior of your soul, Jesus Christ. And here's the best news of all: He's already done the rescuing by dying on the cross for our sins! He's the *true* white knight, who secured your eternity in heaven. Stop waiting; seek His face today!

Jesus, I praise You because You are the rescuer of my soul.
Remind me of this fact when I'm looking for relief in other
people and places. You take care of my present and
eternal needs, and for that I am grateful. Amen.

Is Anyone Listening?

And I will ask the Father, and He will give you
another Comforter (Counselor, Helper, Intercessor,
Advocate, Strengthener, and Standby),
that He may remain with you forever.

JOHN 14:16 AMPC

Our heavenly Father wants to hear from us. He cares so much that He sent the Holy Spirit to be our Counselor, our Comforter. When we pray—when we tell God our needs and give Him praise—He listens. Then He directs the Spirit within us to speak to our hearts and give us reassurance. Our world is filled with noise and distractions. Look for a place where you can be undisturbed for a few minutes. Take a deep breath, lift your prayers, and listen. God will speak—and your heart will hear.

Dear Lord, I thank You for Your care.
Help me to recognize Your voice and to listen well.

A Comfortable Place

Don't you realize that your body is the temple
of the Holy Spirit, who lives in you and was given
to you by God? You do not belong to yourself.

1 CORINTHIANS 6:19 NLT

We take the time to make our homes comfortable and beautiful when we know visitors are coming. In the same way, we ought to prepare our hearts for the Holy Spirit, who lives inside of us. We should daily ask God to help us clean up the junk in our hearts. We should take special care to tune up our bodies through exercise, eating healthful foods, and dressing attractively and modestly. Our bodies belong to God. Taking care of ourselves shows others that we honor God enough to respect and use wisely what He has given us.

Dear Lord, thank You for letting me belong to You.
May my body be a comfortable place for You. Amen.

One Thing Is Needed

"Martha, Martha," the Lord answered,
"you are worried and upset about many things,
but few things are needed—or indeed only one."
LUKE 10:41–42 NIV

We are each given twenty-four hours in a day. Einstein and Edison were given no more than Joseph and Jeremiah of the Old Testament. Since God has blessed each of us with twenty-four hours, let's seek His direction on how to spend this invaluable commodity wisely—giving more to people than things, spending more time on relationships than the rat race. In Luke, our Lord reminded dear, dogged, drained Martha that only one thing is needed—Him.

Father God, oftentimes I get caught up in the minutia of life.
The piled laundry can appear more important than
the precious little ones You've given me. Help me to use my
time wisely. Open my eyes to see what is truly important.

Who Helps the Helper?

The LORD is my strength and my shield; my heart trusted in him, and I am helped: therefore my heart greatly rejoiceth; and with my song will I praise him.

PSALM 28:7 KJV

Helping can be exhausting. The needs of young children, teens, grandchildren, aging parents, neighbors, and fellow church members—the list is never-ending—can stretch us until we're ready to snap. And then we find that *we* need help. Who helps the helper? The Lord does. When we are weak, He is strong. When we are vulnerable, He is our shield. When we can no longer trust in our own resources, we can trust in Him. He is always there, ready to help. Rejoice in Him and praise His name, and you will find the strength to go on.

Father, I'm worn out. I can't care for all the people and needs You bring into my life by myself. I need Your strength. Thank You for being my helper and my shield.

Magnifying Life

My soul makes its boast in the LORD; let the humble
hear and be glad. Oh, magnify the LORD with me,
and let us exalt his name together!

PSALM 34:2–3 ESV

Jesus' mother Mary knew she was the object of God's favor and mercy. That knowledge produced humility. Try as we might, we can't produce this humility in ourselves. It is our natural tendency to be self-promoters. . .to better our own reputations. We need the help of the Spirit to remind us that God has favored each of us with His presence. He did not have to come to us in Christ, but He did. He has chosen to set His love on us. His life redeemed ours, and He sanctifies us. We are recipients of the action of His grace.

Christ Jesus, help me to remember what You have done
for me and desire for others to see and know You.

No More Sting

O death, where is thy sting?
O grave, where is thy victory?

1 CORINTHIANS 15:55 KJV

We have a choice to make. We can either live life in fear or live life by faith. Fear and faith cannot coexist. Jesus Christ has conquered our greatest fear—death. He rose victorious and has given us eternal life through faith. Knowing this truth enables us to courageously face our fears. There is no fear that cannot be conquered by faith. Let's not panic but trust the Lord instead. Let's live by faith and experience the victory that has been given to us through Jesus Christ our Lord.

Lord, You alone know my fears. Help me to trust You more. May I walk in the victory that You have purchased for me. Amen.

Well Watered

*The LORD will guide you always; he will satisfy your
needs in a sun-scorched land and will strengthen
your frame. You will be like a well-watered garden,
like a spring whose waters never fail.*

ISAIAH 58:11 NIV

We need a downpour of God's Word and the Holy Spirit's
presence in our parched spirits. Not an occasional sprinkle,
but a soul soaking to replenish our frazzled bodies and weary
minds. We know this soaking comes from consistent Bible
study, the necessary pruning of confessed sin, and prayer
time. These produce a well-watered garden, fruitful and lush,
mirroring God's beauty, creating a life to which others are
drawn to come and linger in His refreshing presence.

---

*Eternal Father, strengthen my frame, guide my paths,
and satisfy my needs as only You can. Make my life a
well-watered garden, fruitful for You and
Your purposes. Amen.*

A Better Offer

So in everything, do to others what you
would have them do to you.

MATTHEW 7:12 NIV

Jesus took responsibilities, commitments, and obligations seriously. In fact, Jesus said, "All you need to say is simply 'Yes' or 'No'; anything beyond this comes from the evil one" (Matthew 5:37 NIV). Satan desires for us to be stressed out, overcommitted, and not able to do anything well. Satan delights when we treat others in an unkind, offensive manner. However, upon request God will help us prioritize our commitments so that our "yes" is "yes" and our "no" is "no." Then in everything we do, we are liberated to do to others as we would have them do to us.

Lord, please prioritize my commitments to enable me
in everything to do to others as I would desire
for them to do to me. Amen.

Put on a Happy Face

*He restoreth my soul: he leadeth me in the paths
of righteousness for his name's sake.*

PSALM 23:3 KJV

Our God is not a God of negativity but of possibility. He will guide us through our difficulties and beyond them. Today we should turn our thoughts and prayers toward Him. Focus on a hymn or a praise song and play it in your mind. Praise chases away the doldrums and tips our lips up in a smile. With a renewed spirit of optimism and hope we can thank the Giver of all things good. Thankfulness to the Father can turn our plastic smiles into real ones, and as the psalm states, our souls will be restored.

*Father, I'm down in the dumps today. You are my
unending source of strength. Gather me in
Your arms for always. Amen.*

One Step at a Time

With your help I can advance against a troop;
with my God I can scale a wall.

PSALM 18:29 NIV

We often become discouraged when we face a mountain-size task. Whether it's weight loss or a graduate degree or our income taxes, some things just seem impossible. And they often *can't* be done—not all at once. Tasks like these are best faced one step at a time. One pound at a time. Chipping away instead of moving the whole mountain at once. With patience, perseverance, and help from God, your goals may be more attainable than you think.

Dear Father, the task before me seems impossible.
However, I know I can do it with Your help. I pray that
I will trust You every step of the way. Amen.

Mirror Image

Behold, thou art fair, my love;
behold, thou art fair; thou hast doves' eyes.
SONG OF SOLOMON 1:15 KJV

No matter how hard we try, when the focus is on self, we see shortcomings. Our only hope is to see ourselves through a different mirror. We must remember that as we grow as Christians we take on the characteristics of Christ. The more we become like Him, the more beautiful we are in our own eyes and to those around us. God loves to behold us when we are covered in Christ. The mirror image He sees has none of the blemishes or imperfections—only the beauty.

Oh God, thank You for beholding me as being fair and valuable. Help me to see myself through Your eyes. Amen.

Stop and Consider

Listen to this, Job; stop and consider God's wonders.
Do you know how God controls the clouds and makes his
lightning flash? Do you know how the clouds hang poised,
those wonders of him who has perfect knowledge?

JOB 37:14–16 NIV

"Stop and consider My wonders," God told Job. Then He pointed to ordinary observations of the natural world surrounding Job—the clouds that hung poised in the sky, the flashes of lightning. "Not so very ordinary" was God's lesson. Maybe He was trying to remind us that there is no such thing as ordinary. Let's open our eyes and see the wonders around us.

O Father, teach me to stop and consider the ordinary
moments of my life as reminders of You. Help me not
to overlook Your daily care and provisions,
which surround my day. Amen.

Rejoicing with Friends

*Then he calls his friends and neighbors together
and says, "Rejoice with me; I have found my lost sheep."*
LUKE 15:6 NIV

Think of all the reasons you have to celebrate. Are you in good health? Have you overcome a tough obstacle? Are you handling your finances without much grief? Doing well at your job? Bonding with friends or family? If so, then throw yourself a party and invite a friend. Better yet, call your friends and neighbors together, as the scripture indicates. Share your praises with people who will truly appreciate all that the Lord is doing in your life. Let the party begin!

---

*Lord, thank You that I'm created in the image of a God
who knows how to celebrate. I have so many reasons to
rejoice today. Thank You for Your many blessings.
And today I especially want to thank You for
giving me friends to share my joys and sorrows.*

Why Me?

I am Alpha and Omega, the beginning and the
ending, saith the Lord, which is, and which was,
and which is to come, the Almighty.

REVELATION 1:8 KJV

When God spoke our world into existence, He called into being a certain reality, knowing then everything that ever was to happen—and everyone who ever was to be. That you exist now is cause for rejoicing! God made *you* to fellowship with Him! If that fellowship demands trials for a season, rejoice that God thinks you worthy to share in the sufferings of Christ—and, eventually, in His glory. Praise His holy name!

Father, I thank You for giving me this difficult time
in my life. Shine through all my trials today.
I want You to get the glory.

Faith, the Emotional Balancer

*No man is justified by the law in the sight of God,
it is evident: for, The just shall live by faith.*
GALATIANS 3:11 KJV

Emotions mislead us. One day shines with promise as we bounce out of bed in song, while the next day dims in despair and we'd prefer to hide under the bedcovers. It has been said that faith is the bird that feels the light and sings to greet the dawn while it is still dark. The Bible instructs us to live by faith—not by feelings. Faith assures us that daylight will dawn in our darkest moments, affirming God's presence, so that even when we fail to pray and positive feelings fade, our moods surrender to song.

Heavenly Father, I desire for my faith, not my emotions, to dictate my life. I pray for balance in my hide-under-the-cover days, so that I might surrender to You in song. Amen.

Choose Life

The thief comes only to steal and kill and destroy;
I have come that they may have life, and have it to the full.

JOHN 10:10 NIV

God's Word, shows us the lie—and the "liar"—behind defeating thoughts. We have an enemy who delights in our believing negative things, an enemy who wants only destruction for our souls. But Jesus came to give us life! We only have to choose it as an act of the will blended with faith. When we rely on Him alone, He'll enable us to not only survive but *thrive* in our daily routine. Each day, let's make a conscious decision to take hold of what Christ offers us—life to the full.

Loving Lord, help me daily to choose You and the life
You want to give me. Give me the eyes of faith to
trust that You will enable me to serve lovingly.

Follow the Lord's Footsteps

"Come, follow me," Jesus said,
"and I will send you out to fish for people."
MATTHEW 4:19 NIV

Jesus asked His disciples to follow Him, and He asks us to do the same. Following Jesus requires staying right on His heels. We need to be close enough to hear His whisper. Stay close to His heart by opening the Bible daily. Allow His Word to speak to your heart and give you direction. Throughout the day, offer up prayers for guidance and wisdom. Keep in step with Him, and His close presence will bless you beyond measure.

Dear Lord, grant me the desire to follow You.
Help me not to run ahead or lag behind. Amen.

Annual or Perennial?

*They are like trees planted along the riverbank,
bearing fruit each season. Their leaves never wither,
and they prosper in all they do.*

PSALM 1:3 NLT

Annuals or perennials? Each has its advantages. Annuals are inexpensive, provide instant gratification, and keep boredom from setting in. Perennials require an initial investment but, when properly tended, faithfully provide beauty year after year—long after the annuals have dried up and withered away. Perennials are designed for the long haul—not just short-term enjoyment but long-term beauty. The application to our lives is two-fold. First, be a perennial—long lasting, enduring, slow growing, steady, and faithful. Second, don't be discouraged by your inevitable dormant seasons. Tend to your soul, and it will reward you with years of lush blossoms.

Father, be the gardener of my soul. Amen.

Have You Looked Up?

The heavens proclaim the glory of God. The skies display his craftsmanship. Day after day they continue to speak; night after night they make him known.

PSALM 19:1–2 NLT

God has placed glimpses of creation's majesty—evidence of His love—throughout our world. Sunsets, seashells, flowers, snowflakes, changing seasons, moonlit shadows. Such glories are right in front of us every single day! But we must develop eyes to see these reminders in our daily life and not let the cares and busyness of our lives keep our heads turned down. Have you looked up today?

Lord, open my eyes! Unstuff my ears! Teach me to see the wonders of Your creation every day and to point them out to my children.

Faultless

*To him who is able to keep you from stumbling
and to present you before his glorious presence
without fault and with great joy.*

JUDE 1:24 NIV

Jesus loves us so much despite our shortcomings. He is
the One who can keep us from falling—who can present us
faultless before the Father. Because of this we can have our
joy restored no matter what. Whether we have done wrong
and denied it or have been falsely accused, we can come
into His presence to be restored and lifted up. Let us keep
our eyes on Him instead of on our need to justify ourselves
to God or others.

*Thank You, Jesus, for Your cleansing love
and for the joy we can find in Your presence. Amen.*

Reflecting God in Our Work

Whatever you do, work at it with all your heart,
as working for the Lord, not for human masters.

COLOSSIANS 3:23 NIV

As believers, we are God's children. No one is perfect, and for this there is grace. However, we may be the only reflection of our heavenly Father that some will ever see. Our attitudes and actions on the job speak volumes to those around us. Although it may be tempting to do just enough to get by, we put forth our best effort when we remember we represent God to the world. A Christian's character on the job should be a positive reflection of the Lord.

Father, help me today to represent You well through my
work. I want to reflect Your love in all I do. Amen.

Just Half a Cup

*I am coming to you now, but I say these things while
I am still in the world, so that they may have
the full measure of my joy within them.*

JOHN 17:13 NIV

Our heavenly Father longs to bestow His richest blessings
and wisdom on us. He loves us, so He desires to fill our cup
to overflowing with the things that He knows will bring us
pleasure and growth. Do you tell Him to stop pouring when
your cup is only half full? You may not even realize it, but
perhaps your actions dictate that your cup remain half empty.
Seek a full cup and enjoy the full measure of the joy of the Lord.

*Dear Jesus, forgive me for not accepting the fullness of
Your blessings and Your joy. Help me to see the ways that
I prevent my cup from being filled to overflowing. Thank You
for wanting me to have the fullness of Your joy. Amen.*

53

Hide and Seek

And do you seek great things for yourself?
Seek them not, for behold, I am bringing disaster
upon all flesh, declares the LORD.

JEREMIAH 45:5 ESV

God warns us: *Don't seek great things.* The more we seek them, the more elusive they become. As soon as we think we have them in our grasp, they disappear. If we commit to more activities than we can realistically handle, the best result is that we can't follow through. Worse, we might make them our god. Jesus tells us what we should seek: the kingdom of God and His righteousness (Matthew 6:33). When we seek the right things, He'll give us every good and perfect gift (James 1:17). And that will be more than we can ask for or dream of.

Lord, please teach me to seek not greatness
but You. May You be the all in all of my life.

Location, Location, Location

Those who live in the shelter of the Most High will find
rest in the shadow of the Almighty. This I declare about
the LORD: he alone is my refuge, my place of
safety; he is my God, and I trust him.

PSALM 91:1–2 NLT

If something is getting you down in life, check your location.
Where are your thoughts? Let what the world has conditioned
you to think go in one ear and out the other. Stand on the
truth, the promises of God's Word. Say of the Lord, "God is
my refuge! I am hidden in Christ! Nothing can harm me. In
Him I trust!" Say it loud. Say it often. Say it over and over until
it becomes your reality. And you will find yourself dwelling
in that secret place every moment of the day.

God, You are my refuge. When I abide in You,
nothing can harm me. Your Word is the truth on which
I rely. Fill me with Your light and the peace of Your
love. It's You and me, Lord, all the way! Amen.

Light My Path

Your word is a lamp for my feet, a light on my path.
PSALM 119:105 NIV

God's Word is like a streetlamp. Often we *think* we know where we're going and where the stumbling blocks are. We believe we can avoid pitfalls and maneuver the path successfully on our own. But the truth is that without God's Word, we are walking in darkness, stumbling and tripping. When we sincerely begin to search God's Word, we find the path becomes clear. God's light allows us to live our lives in the most fulfilling way possible, a way planned out from the very beginning by God Himself.

Jesus, shine Your light upon my path. I have spent too long wandering through the darkness, looking for my way. As I search Your Word, I ask You to make it a lamp to my feet so that I can avoid the pitfalls of the world and walk safely along the path You have created specifically for me.

Power Up

The Spirit of God,
who raised Jesus from the dead, lives in you.

ROMANS 8:11 NLT

God is the same yesterday, today, and forever. His strength does not diminish over time. That same mountain-moving power you read about in the lives of people from the Old and New Testaments still exists today. We don't have to go it alone. Our heavenly Father wants to help. All we have to do is ask. He has already made His power available to His children. Whatever we face, wherever we go, whatever dreams we have for our lives—we take courage and know that anything is possible when we draw on the power of God.

Father, help me to remember that You are always with me,
ready to help me do all things. Amen.

Comfort Food

For whatever things were written before were
written for our learning, that we through the patience
and comfort of the Scriptures might have hope.

ROMANS 15:4 NKJV

Romans 15:4 tells us that the scriptures are comfort food for the soul. They were written and given so that through our learning we would be comforted with the truths of God. Worldly pleasures bring a temporary comfort, but the problem still remains when the pleasure or comfort fades. However, the words of God are soothing and provide permanent hope and peace. Through God's Word, you will be changed and your troubles will dim in the bright light of Christ. So the next time you are sad, lonely, or disappointed, turn to the Word of God as your source of comfort.

Thank You, Father, for the rich comfort Your Word provides.
Help me to remember to find my comfort in scripture
rather than through earthly things that will
ultimately fail me. Amen.

Power of the Word

The Spirit gives life; the flesh counts for nothing.
The words I have spoken to you—
they are full of the Spirit and life.

JOHN 6:63 NIV

Jesus told His followers that His words were full of the Spirit and life. When we hear His Word, meditate on it, pray it, memorize it, and ask for faith to believe it, He comes to us in it and transforms our lives through it. Once the Word is in our mind or before our eyes and ears, the Holy Spirit can work it into our hearts and our consciences. Jesus told us to abide in His Word—putting ourselves in a place to hear and receive the Word. The rest is the beautiful and mysterious work of the Spirit.

Thank You, Jesus, the Living Word, for changing my heart and my mind through the power of Your Word.

Can God Interrupt You?

In their hearts humans plan their course,
but the LORD established their steps.

PROVERBS 16:9 NIV

Have you ever considered that perhaps God has ordained your interruptions? Perhaps, just perhaps, God may be trying to get your attention. There is nothing wrong with planning our day. However, we have such limited vision. God sees the big picture. Be open. Be flexible. Allow God to change your plans in order to accomplish His divine purposes. Instead of becoming frustrated, look for ways the Lord might be working. Be willing to join Him. When we do, interruptions become blessings.

Dear Lord, forgive me when I am so rigidly locked into my own agenda that I miss Yours. Give me Your eternal perspective so that I may be open to divine interruptions. Amen.

Marvelous Thunder

God's voice thunders in marvelous ways;
he does great things beyond our understanding.

JOB 37:5 NIV

Have you ever reflected deeply on the power that God is?
Not that He *has*, but that He *is*. Consider this: The One who
controls nature also holds every one of our tears in His hand.
He is our Father, and He works on our behalf. He is more than
enough to meet our needs; He does things far beyond what our
human minds can understand. This One, who is power, loves
you. He looks at you and says, "I delight in you, My daughter."
Wow! His ways are marvelous and beyond understanding.

Lord God, You are power. You hold all things in Your hand,
and You chose to love me. You see my actions, hear my
thoughts, watch my heartbreaks. . .and You still love me.
Please help me trust in Your power, never my own.

Eye Care

For thus says the LORD of hosts. . .
"he who touches you touches the apple of His eye."
ZECHARIAH 2:8 NKJV

To think that we are the apple of God's eye is incredible. Consider the care He must take for us. He will go to great lengths to protect us from harm. When something or someone does attack us, God feels our pain. He is instantly aware of our discomfort, for it is His own. When the storms of life come, we must remember that God feels each twinge of suffering. Despite the adversity, we can praise God, for He is sheltering us.

Thank You, God, that You are so aware of what is happening to me. Thank You for Your protection. Amen.

God's Mountain Sanctuary

*And seeing the multitudes, he went up into a
mountain. . .and. . .his disciples came unto him:
and he opened his mouth, and taught them.*

MATTHEW 5:1-2 KJV

Jesus often retreated to a mountain to pray. There He called
His disciples to depart from the multitudes so that He could
teach them valuable truths—the lessons we learn from nature.
Do you yearn for a place where problems evaporate like the
morning dew? Do you need a place of solace? God is wherever
you are—behind a bedroom door, nestled alongside you in
your favorite chair, or even standing at a sink full of dirty
dishes. Come away and enter God's mountain sanctuary.

*Heavenly Father, I long to hear Your voice and to walk
in the path You clear before me. Help me to find
sanctuary in Your abiding presence. Amen.*

A Fragrant Offering

*Follow God's example, therefore, as dearly loved
children and walk in the way of love, just as Christ
loved us and gave himself up for us as a
fragrant offering and sacrifice to God.*

EPHESIANS 5:1-2 NIV

If we carry the scent of Christ in our daily walk, people will
be drawn to us and want to "stay for a while." But how do we
give off that amazing, inviting fragrance? There's really only
one way—by imitating God. By loving others fully. By seeing
them through His eyes. By looking with great compassion
on those who are hurting, as Jesus did when He went about
healing the sick and pouring out His life for those in need.
As we live a life of love in front of those we care for, we exude
the sweetest fragrance of all—Christ.

*Dear Lord, I long to live a life that points people to You.
As I care for those in need, may the sweet-smelling
aroma of You and Your love be an invitation
for people to draw near.*

Masterpiece

*You made all the delicate, inner parts of my body
and knit me together in my mother's womb.*

PSALM 139:13 NLT

At the moment of your conception, roughly three million decisions were made about you. Everything from your eye color to the shape of your nose and the swirl of your fingerprints was determined in the blink of an eye. God is a big God. Unfathomable. Incomparable. Frankly, words just don't do Him justice. And He made *you*. You were knit together by a one-of-a-kind, amazing God who is absolutely, undeniably, head-over-heels crazy-in-love with you. Try to wrap your brain around that.

---

*Heavenly Father and Creator, thank You for the
amazing gift of life, for my uniqueness and individuality.
Help me to use my life as a gift of praise to You. Amen.*

How About Some Fun?

A twinkle in the eye means joy in the heart,
and good news makes you feel fit as a fiddle.

PROVERBS 15:30 MSG

God does not want His kids to be worn out and stressed out.
A little relaxation, recreation—and, yes—*fun* are essential
components of a balanced life. Even Jesus and His disciples
found it necessary to get away from the crowds and pressures
of ministry to rest. There's a lot of fun to be had out there—
playing tennis or golf, jogging, swimming, painting, knitting,
playing a musical instrument, visiting an art gallery, enjoying
a board game, or going to a movie, a play, or a football game.
Have you had any fun this week?

Lord, You are the One who gives balance to my life.
Help me to find time today for a little relaxation,
recreation, and even fun. Amen.

Ladies in Waiting

I will wait for the LORD. . . . I will put my trust in him.
ISAIAH 8:17 NIV

Do we want joy without accepting heartache? Peace without living through the stress? Patience without facing demands? God sees things differently. He's giving us the opportunity to learn through these delays, irritations, and struggles. Like Isaiah, we need to learn the art of waiting on God. He will come through every time—but in *His* time, not ours. The wait may be hours or days, or it could be years. But God is always faithful to provide for us. It is when we learn to wait on Him that we will find joy, peace, and patience through the struggle.

Father, You know what I need, so I will wait. Help me be patient, knowing that You control my situation and that all good things come in Your time.

When I Think of the Heavens

When I consider your heavens, the work of your fingers,
the moon and the stars, which you have set in place,
what is mankind, that you are mindful of them,
human beings that you care for them?

PSALM 8:3-4 NIV

Daughter of God, you are important to your heavenly Father, more important than the sun, the moon, and the stars. You are created in the image of God, and He cares for you. In fact, He cares so much that He sent His Son, Jesus, to offer His life as a sacrifice for your sins. The next time you look up at the heavens, the next time you *ooh* and *aah* over a majestic mountain or emerald waves crashing against the shoreline, remember that those things, in all of their splendor, don't even come close to you—God's greatest creation.

Oh, Father, who am I that You would think twice about me?
And yet You do. You love me, and for that I'm eternally grateful!

The Dream Maker

*"No eye has seen, no ear has heard. . .no human mind
has conceived"—the things that God has
prepared for those who love him.*

1 CORINTHIANS 2:9 NIV

Dreams, goals, and expectations are part of our daily lives.
We have an idea of what we want and how we're going to
achieve it. Disappointment can raise its ugly head when
what we wanted—what we expected—doesn't happen like we
thought it should or doesn't happen as fast as we planned. God
knows the dreams He has placed inside of you. He created
you and knows what you can do—even better than you know
yourself. Maintain your focus—not on the dream but on the
Dream Maker—and together you will achieve your dream.

*God, thank You for putting dreams in my heart.
I refuse to quit. I'm looking to You to show me
how to reach my dreams. Amen.*

A Heavenly Party

I tell you that in the same way there will be more rejoicing in heaven over one sinner who repents than over ninety-nine righteous persons who do not need to repent.

LUKE 15:7 NIV

The Father threw you your very own party on the moment you accepted His Son as your Savior. Did you experience a taste of that party from the response of your spiritual mentors here on earth? As Christians, we should celebrate with our new brothers and sisters in Christ every chance we get. If you haven't yet taken that step in your faith, don't wait! Heaven's party planners are eager to get your celebration started.

Father, I am so grateful that You rejoice in new Christians. Strengthen my desire to reach the lost while I am here on earth. Then when I reach heaven, the heavenly parties will be all the sweeter! Amen.

Choosing Wisely

Our mouths were filled with laughter.
PSALM 126:2 NIV

We women often plan perfect family events only to find out how imperfectly things can turn out. The soufflé falls, the cat leaps onto the counter and licks the cheeseball, little Johnny drops Aunt Martha's crystal gravy dish (full of gravy, of course). The Bible says that Sarah laughed at the most unexpected, traumatic time of her life—when God announced that she would have a baby at the age of ninety (Genesis 18:12). At this unforeseen turn of events, she could either laugh, cry, or run away screaming. She chose to laugh.

Lord, give us an extra dollop of grace and peace to laugh about unexpected dilemmas that pop up and to remember that our reaction is a choice. Amen.

Anxiety Check!

Do not be anxious about anything,
but in every situation, by prayer and petition,
with thanksgiving, present your requests to God.

PHILIPPIANS 4:6 NIV

Checking to make sure we've locked the door, turned off the stove, and unplugged the curling iron just comes naturally. So why do we forget some of the bigger checks in life? Take anxiety, for instance. When was the last time you did an anxiety check? Days? Weeks? Months? Chances are, you're due for another. After all, we're instructed not to be anxious about anything. Instead, we're to present our requests to God with thanksgiving in our hearts. We're to turn to Him in prayer so that He can take our burdens. Once they've lifted, say bye-bye to anxiety!

Father, I get anxious sometimes. And I don't always remember to turn to You with my anxiety. In fact, I forget to check for anxiety at all. Today I hand my anxieties to You. Thank You that I can present my requests to You.

Difficult People

Do not turn your freedom into an opportunity
for the flesh, but through love serve one another.

GALATIANS 5:13 NASB

Sometimes, like David, we need to turn our skirmishes with others over to the Lord. Then, by using our weapons—God's Word and a steadfast faith—we need to love and forgive others as God loves and forgives us. Although we may not like to admit it, we have *all* said and done some pretty awful things, making the lives of others difficult. Yet God has forgiven us *and* continues to love us. So do the right thing. Pull your feet out of the mire of unforgiveness, sidestep verbal retaliation, and stand tall in the freedom of love and forgiveness.

Father, the words and deeds of others have left me wounded and bleeding. Forgiveness and love seem to be the last thing on my mind. Change my heart, Lord. Help me to love and forgive others as You love and forgive me. Amen.

A Strong Heart

*Whom have I in heaven but you? And earth has nothing
I desire besides you. My flesh and my heart may fail,
but God is the strength of my heart and my portion forever.*
PSALM 73:25-26 NIV

You don't have to be strong. In your weakness, God's strength shines through. And His strength surpasses anything you could produce, even on your best day. It's the same strength that spoke the heavens and the earth into existence. The same strength that parted the Red Sea. And it's the same strength that made the journey up the hill to the cross. So how do you tap into that strength? There's really only one way. Come into His presence. Spend some quiet time with Him. Allow His strong arms to encompass you. God is all you will ever need.

---

*Father, I feel so weak at times. It's hard just to put one
foot in front of the other. But I know You are my strength.
Invigorate me with that strength today, Lord.*

King Forever

You, O God, are my king from ages past,
bringing salvation to the earth.

PSALM 74:12 NLT

Sometimes it seems like every part of our lives is affected by change. Nothing ever seems to stay the same. These changes can leave us feeling unsteady in the present and uncertain about the future. It's different in God's kingdom. He's the King now just as He was in the days of Abraham. His reign will continue until the day His Son returns to earth and then on into eternity. We can rely—absolutely depend on—His unchanging nature. Take comfort in the stability of the King—He's our leader now and forever!

Almighty King, You are my rock. When my world is in
turmoil and changes swirl around me, You are my
anchor and my center of balance. Thank You
for never changing. Amen.

Going Above and Beyond

*Now to him who is able to do immeasurably more
than all we ask or imagine. . .to him be glory in
the church and in Christ Jesus throughout
all generations, for ever and ever!*

EPHESIANS 3:20–21 NIV

Think for a moment. . . What have you asked for? What have
you imagined? It's amazing to think that God—in His infinite
power and wisdom—can do immeasurably more than all that!
How? According to the power that is at work within us. It's not
our power, thankfully. We don't have enough power to scrape
the surface of what we'd like to see done in our lives. But His
power in us gets the job done. . .and more. Praise the Lord!
Praise Him in the church and throughout all generations!
He's an immeasurable God.

*Heavenly Father, it's amazing to realize You have more
power in Your little finger than all of mankind has
put together. Today I praise You for going above
and beyond all I could ask or imagine.*

Put on Love

And over all these virtues put on love,
which binds them all together in perfect unity.

COLOSSIANS 3:14 NIV

There is one accessory that always fits, always looks right, always seems appropriate, and always makes us more attractive to others. When we wear it, we are beautiful. When we wear it, we become more popular, more sought-after, more admired. What is that accessory, you ask, and where can you buy it? It's love, and you can't buy it anywhere. But it's free, and it's always available through the Holy Spirit. When we call on Him to help us love others, He cloaks us in a beautiful covering that draws people to us and makes us perfectly lovely in every way.

Dear Father, as I get dressed each day,
help me to remember the most important
accessory I can wear is Your love.

Cartwheels of Joy

*I'm singing joyful praise to G*OD. . . . *Counting on G*OD's
*Rule to prevail, I take heart and gain strength.
I run like a deer. I feel like I'm king of the mountain!*
HABAKKUK 3:18-19 MSG

What would happen if we followed the advice of the psalmist and turned a cartwheel of joy in our hearts—regardless of the circumstances—then leaned on and trusted in His rule to prevail? Think of the happiness and peace which could be ours with a total surrender to God's care. Taking a giant step, armed with scriptures and praise and joy, we can surmount any obstacle put before us, running like a deer, climbing the tall mountains. With God at our side, it's possible to be king of the mountain.

---

*Dear Lord, I need Your help. Gently guide me
so I might learn to lean on You and become
confident in Your care. Amen.*

Trials and Wisdom

*If any of you lacks wisdom, you should ask
God, who gives generously to all without finding
fault, and it will be given to you.*

JAMES 1:5 NIV

Things won't be easy and simple until we get to heaven. So how can we lift our chins and head into tomorrow without succumbing to discouragement? We remember that God is good. We trust His faithfulness. We ask for His presence and peace during each moment. We pray for wisdom and believe that the God who holds the universe in His hands is working every single trial and triumph together for our good and for His glory. This verse in James tells us that when we lack wisdom we should simply ask God for it! Be encouraged that the Lord will give you wisdom generously without finding fault!

---

*Lord Jesus, please give me wisdom. So many troubles
are weighing me down. Help me give You all my
burdens and increase my faith and trust in You.*

Step-by-Step

For we walk by faith [we regulate our lives and conduct ourselves by our conviction or belief. . .with trust and holy fervor; thus we walk] not by sight or appearance.

2 CORINTHIANS 5:7 AMPC

The experiences and circumstances of our lives can often lead us to lose heart. The apostle Paul exhorts us to look away from this present world and rely on God by faith. Webster's dictionary defines faith as a firm belief and complete trust in something. Trusting when our faith is small is not an easy task. Today, grasp hold of God's Word and feel His presence. Hold tightly and don't let your steps falter. He is beside you and will lead you.

Dear heavenly Father, today I choose to clutch Your Hand and feel Your presence as I trudge the pathways of my life. I trust You are by my side. Amen.

Raise the Roof

Come, let's shout praises to GOD, raise the roof for the Rock
who saved us! Let's march into his presence singing
praises, lifting the rafters with our hymns!

PSALM 95:1-2 MSG

Not many had it rougher than King David, who curled up in
caves to hide from his enemies, or Paul, who was forced to
sit in dark dungeon cells. Yet they still praised God despite
the circumstances. And our God extended His grace to them
as they acclaimed Him in their suffering. The Lord wants to
hear our shouts of joy and see us march into the courtyard
rejoicing. He hears our faltering songs and turns them into
a symphony for His ears. So lift up your voice and join in the
praise to our Creator and Lord.

Dear heavenly Father, I praise Your holy Name.
Bless You, Lord. Thank You for Your grace
and mercy toward me. Amen.

Biblical Encouragement for Your Heart

Don't be concerned about the outward beauty of
fancy hairstyles, expensive jewelry, or beautiful clothes.
You should clothe yourselves instead with the beauty that
comes from within, the unfading beauty of a gentle
and quiet spirit, which is so precious to God.

1 PETER 3:3–4 NLT

God is concerned with what is on the inside. He listens to how you respond to others and watches the facial expressions you choose to exhibit. He sees your heart. The Lord desires that you clothe yourself with a gentle and quiet spirit. He declares this as unfading beauty, the inner beauty of the heart. Focus on this and no one will even notice whether your jewelry shines. Your face will be radiant with the joy of the Lord, and your heart will overflow with grace and peace.

Lord, grant me a quiet and gentle spirit.
I ask this in Jesus' name. Amen.

The Gift of Prayer

First of all, then, I admonish and urge that petitions,
prayers, intercessions, and thanksgivings be offered on
behalf of all men. . . . For such [praying] is good and right,
and [it is] pleasing and acceptable to God our Savior.
1 TIMOTHY 2:1, 3 AMPC

There is such joy in giving gifts. Seeing the delight on someone's face over receiving something unexpected is exciting. Perhaps the absolute greatest gift one person can give to another doesn't come in a box. It can't be wrapped or presented formally; but instead, it is the words spoken to God for someone—the gift of prayer. When we pray for others, we ask God to intervene and to make Himself known to them. We can pray for God's plan and purpose in their lives. We can ask God to bless them or protect them. Who would God have you give the gift of prayer to today?

Lord, thank You for bringing people into my heart
and mind who need prayer. Help me to pray
for the things that they need from You.

Encourage One Another

Therefore encourage one another
and build each other up, just as in fact you are doing.

1 THESSALONIANS 5:11 NIV

Encouragement is more than words. It is also valuing, being tolerant of, serving, and praying for one another. It is looking for what is good and strong in a person and celebrating it. Encouragement means sincerely forgiving and asking for forgiveness, recognizing someone's weaknesses and holding out a helping hand, giving humbly while building someone up, helping others to hope in the Lord, and praying that God will encourage them in ways that you cannot. Whom will you encourage today? Get in the habit of encouraging others. It will bless them and you.

Heavenly Father, open my eyes to those who need
encouragement. Show me how I can help. Amen.

Joyous Light

Whom having not seen, ye love; in whom, though now ye see him not, yet believing, ye rejoice with joy unspeakable and full of glory.

1 PETER 1:8 KJV

Jesus is the Light of the World. When we accept Him, the light is poured into us. The Holy Spirit comes to reside within, bringing His light. A glorious gift graciously given to us. When we realize the importance of the gift and the blessings that result from a life led by the Father, we can't contain our happiness. The joy and hope that fill our hearts well up. Joy uncontained comes when Jesus becomes our Lord. Through Him, through faith, we have hope for the future. What joy! So let it spill forth in love.

*Lord, help me to be a light unto the world,
shining forth Your goodness. Amen.*

He Carries Us

In his love and mercy he redeemed them.
He lifted them up and carried them through all the years.

ISAIAH 63:9-10 NLT

Are you feeling broken today? Depressed? Defeated? Run to Jesus, not away from Him. He will carry us—no matter what pain we have to endure. No matter what happens to us. God sent Jesus to be our Redeemer. He knew the world would hate, malign, and kill Jesus. Yet He allowed His very flesh to writhe in agony on the cross so that we could also become His sons and daughters. He loved me—and you—that much.

Lord Jesus, thank You for coming to us—for not abandoning
us when we are broken. Thank You for Your work on the
cross; for Your grace, mercy, and love. Help me to seek
You even when I can't feel You; to love You even
when I don't know all the answers.

Linking Hearts with God

*You will receive power when the Holy Spirit comes on you;
and you will be my witnesses. . .to the ends of the earth.*

ACTS 1:8 NIV

God knows our hearts. He knows what we need to make it through a day. So in His kindness, He gave us a gift in the form of the Holy Spirit. As a Counselor, a Comforter, and a Friend, the Holy Spirit acts as our inner compass. He upholds us when times are hard and helps us hear God's directions. When the path of obedience grows dark, the Spirit floods it with light. What revelation! He lives within us. Therefore, our prayers are lifted to the Father, to the very throne of God!

*Father God, how blessed I am to come into Your presence.
Help me, Father, when I am weak. Guide me this day. Amen.*

A Woman of Worth

A wife of noble character who can find? She is worth far more than rubies. Her husband has full confidence in her and lacks nothing of value. She brings him good, not harm, all the days of her life.

PROVERBS 31:10-12 NIV

Are you the woman of worth that Jesus intends you to be? We often don't think we are. Between running a household, rushing to work, taking care of the children, volunteering for worthwhile activities, and still being a role model for our families, we think we've failed miserably. Sometimes we don't fully realize that learning to be a noble woman of character takes time. Our experiences can be offered to another generation seeking wisdom from others who have "been there." You are a woman of worth. God said so!

Father God, thank You for equipping me to be a woman of noble character. I love You, Lord, and I will continue to put You first in my life. Amen.

Like Little Children

Some people brought their little children to Jesus so he
could touch them, but his followers told them to stop.
When Jesus saw this, he was upset and said to them...
"Don't stop them, because the kingdom of God belongs
to people who are like these children. I tell you the truth,
you must accept the kingdom of God as if you were
a little child, or you will never enter it."

MARK 10:13–15 NCV

This passage in Mark tells us that no matter how old we
are, God wants us to come to Him with the faith of a child.
He wants us to be open and honest about our feelings. He
wants us to trust Him wholeheartedly, just like little kids do.
As adults, we sometimes play games with God. We tell God
what we think He wants to hear, forgetting that He already
knows our hearts! God is big enough to handle your honesty.
Tell Him how you really feel.

Father, help me come to You as a little child
and be more open and honest with You in prayer.

Loving Sisters

But Ruth replied, "Don't urge me to leave you or
to turn back from you. Where you go I will go,
and where you stay I will stay. Your people will
be my people and your God my God."

RUTH 1:16 NIV

The story of Ruth and Naomi is inspiring on many levels. Both women realized that their commitment, friendship, and love for each other surpassed any of their differences. They were a blessing to each other. Do you have girlfriends who would do almost anything for you? A true friendship is a gift from God. Those relationships provide us with love, companionship, encouragement, loyalty, honesty, understanding, and more! Lasting friendships are essential to living a balanced life.

Father God, thank You for giving us the gift of friendship.
May I be the blessing to my girlfriends that they are to me.
Please help me to always encourage and love them and to
be a loving support for them in both their trials and their
times of happiness. I praise You for my loving sisters! Amen.

Breath of Life

He heals the brokenhearted and binds up their wounds
[curing their pains and their sorrows].

PSALM 147:3 AMPC

When your life brings moments of disappointment, hurt, and pain that are almost unbearable, remember that you serve the One who heals hearts. He knows you best and loves you most. When the wind is knocked out of you and you feel like there is no oxygen left in the room, let God provide you with the air you need to breathe. Breathe out a prayer to Him, and breathe in His peace and comfort today.

Lord, be my breath of life today and always.

High Expectations

"They found grace out in the desert. . . . Israel, out looking
for a place to rest, met God out looking for them!"
God told them, "I've never quit loving you and
never will. Expect love, love, and more love!"

JEREMIAH 31:2–3 MSG

Despite their transgressions, God told the Israelites He never quit loving them. That is true for you today. Look beyond any circumstances and you will discover God looking at you, His eyes filled with love. Scripture promises an overwhelming, unexpected river of love that will pour out when we trust the Lord our God. Rest today in His word. Expect God's love, love, and more love to fill that empty place in your life.

Father, we read these words and choose
this day to believe in Your unfailing love. Amen.

A Continual Feast

The cheerful heart has a continual feast.
PROVERBS 15:15 NIV

Our choice of companions has much to do with our outlook. Negativity and positivity are both contagious. The writer of Proverbs says that a cheerful heart has a continual feast. So it's safe to assume that a grumpy heart will feel hungry and lacking instead of feeling full. While God calls us to minister to those who are hurting, we can do so with discernment. Next time someone complains, ask them to pray with you about their concerns. Tell them a story of how you overcame negativity or repaired a relationship. You might help turn their day around!

God, help me be a positive influence on my friends and family. Give me wisdom and the unwavering hope that comes from Christ, that I may share Your joy with others.

A Good Morsel

Taste and see that the LORD is good;
blessed is the one who takes refuge in him.

PSALM 34:8 NIV

The world gives the idea to nonbelievers that God isn't worth a taste. The world emphasizes a self-focus, while the Lord says to put others before self and God before all. In reality, walking and talking with God is the best thing you can do for yourself. Like so many foods that are good for us, all our spiritual life requires is that first taste, a tiny morsel, which whets the appetite for more of Him. Then you can be open to all the goodness, all the fullness of the Lord.

Lord, fill my cup to overflowing with Your love
so that it pours out of me in a way that makes
others want what I have. Amen.

Be Happy!

Blessed are those who act justly,
who always do what is right.
PSALM 106:3 NIV

In the world that we live in today, some might think that a bank error or a mistake on a bill in their favor would be justification for keeping the money without a word. But a true Christ-follower would not look at these kinds of situations as good or fortunate events. Our happiness is in being honest and doing what is right, because that happiness is the promised spiritual reward. Because we want to be blessed by God—to be a happy follower of Him—we will seek to always do what is right.

Gracious and heavenly Father, thank You for Your blessings
each and every day. I am thankful to be Your follower.
When I am tempted to do something that would displease
You, remind me that You will bless me if I act justly.
My happiness will be a much better reward.
In Your Name, amen.

95

Your Heavenly Father

The LORD's love never ends; his mercies never stop.
They are new every morning; LORD, your loyalty is great.
LAMENTATIONS 3:22-23 NCV

Regardless of your relationship with your earthly father, your heavenly Father loves you with an *unfailing love*. He is faithful to walk with you through the ups and downs of life. Remember that every day is a day to honor your heavenly Father. Begin and end today praising Him for who he is. Express thanksgiving. Present your requests to Him. Tell Him how much you love Him. God longs to be your Abba Father, a loving Daddy to you, His daughter!

Father, for some, today is a happy occasion. For others,
it stings a bit. Thank You that You are a loving God,
my Abba Father, my Redeemer. Amen.

Start Your Day with God

*In the morning, Lord, you hear my voice; in the morning
I lay my requests before you and wait expectantly.*

PSALM 5:3 NIV

As you wake up in the morning, thank the Lord for a new day.
Ask Him to control your thoughts and attitude as you make the
bed. Thank Him for providing for you as you toast your bagel.
Ask that your self-image be based on your relationship with
Christ as you get dressed and brush your teeth. Continue to
pray as you drive to work or school. Spend time in His Word
throughout the day. Then end your day by thanking Him for
His love and faithfulness.

---

*Dear Lord, thank You for the gift of a new day.
Help me be aware of Your constant presence in my life.*

Listening Closely

I will listen to what God the LORD says.
PSALM 85:8 NIV

Listening is a learned art too often forgotten in the busyness of a day. The alarm clock buzzes and we hit the floor running, toss out a prayer, maybe sing a song of praise, grab our car keys, and are out the door. If only we'd slow down and let the heavenly Father's words sink into our spirits, what a difference we might see in our prayer life. This day, stop. Listen. See what God has in store for you.

Lord, how I want to surrender and seek Your will!
Please still my spirit and speak to me. Amen.

Pray about Everything

The LORD directs the steps of the godly.
He delights in every detail of their lives.
PSALM 37:23 NLT

The Bible says that the Lord delights in every detail of His children's lives. Adult prayers don't have to be well-ordered and formal. God loves hearing His children's voices, and no detail is too little or dull to pray about. Tell God that you hope the coffeehouse will have your favorite pumpkin-spice latte on its menu. Ask Him to give you patience as you wait in line. Thank Him for how wonderful that coffee tastes! Get into the habit of talking with Him all day long, because He loves you and delights in all facets of your life.

Dear God, teach me to pray about everything
with childlike innocence and faith. Amen.

A Joyful Heart

*Sarah said, "God has brought me laughter, and everyone
who hears about this will laugh with me."*

GENESIS 21:6 NIV

In the Bible, King Solomon says, "Every day is hard for
those who suffer, but a happy heart is like a continual feast"
(Proverbs 15:15 NCV). Are you or someone you know unhappy?
A little laughter might help. Begin with a smile. When you hear
laughter, move toward it and try to join in. Seek the company
of happy friends, and invite humor into your conversations.
Most of all, praise God. Praise is the best way to heal a hurting
soul. Praise God joyfully for His many blessings.

---

*Lord, whenever my heart is heavy,
encourage me to heal it with joy. Amen.*

Fix Your Thoughts on Truth

*Fix your thoughts on what is true, and honorable,
and right, and pure, and lovely, and admirable.*

PHILIPPIANS 4:8 NLT

Dig through the scriptures and find truths from God's Word to combat any false message that you may be struggling with. Write them down and memorize them. Here are a few to get started:

- God looks at my heart, not my outward appearance. (1 Samuel 16:7)
- I am free in Christ. (1 Corinthians 1:30)
- I am a new creation. My old self is gone! (2 Corinthians 5:17)

The next time you feel negativity slip into your thinking, fix your thoughts on what you know to be true. Pray and ask the Lord to replace the doubts with His words of truth.

---

*Lord God, please help me control my thoughts and
set my mind and heart on You alone.*

The Simple Things

In him our hearts rejoice, for we trust in his holy name.

PSALM 33:21 NIV

God knows all the simple pleasures you enjoy—and He created them for your delight. When the simple things that can come only by His hand fill you with contentment, He is pleased. He takes pleasure in you. You are His delight. Giving you peace, comfort, and a sense of knowing that you belong to Him is a simple thing for Him. Take a moment today and step away from the busyness of life. Take notice and fully experience some of those things you enjoy most. Then share that special joy with Him.

Lord, thank You for the simple things that bring pleasure to my day. I enjoy each gift You've given me. I invite You to share those moments with me today.

Encourage Others

Worry weighs a person down;
an encouraging word cheers a person up.

PROVERBS 12:25 NLT

There is so much sorrow in this world. At any given time, there are many people within your sphere of influence who are hurting. Worry weighs them down as they face disappointment, loss, and other trials. Think about how much it means to you when someone takes the time to encourage you. Do the same for others. Be the voice of encouragement. There is blessing to be found in lifting up those around you.

Father, as I go through this week, make me an encourager.
Provide opportunities for me to encourage those
around me. I truly desire to cheer up the hearts
of those who are worried. Amen.

Whispers in the Wind

*Then Jesus told him, "Because you have seen me,
you have believed; blessed are those who have
not seen and yet have believed."*

JOHN 20:29 NIV

We can't see God. We can't take Him by the hand or even
converse with Him face-to-face like we do a friend. But we still
know He is present in our lives because we can experience
the effects. God moves among His people, and we can see
it. God speaks to His people, and we can hear the still, small
voice. And, just as we can feel the wind across our cheeks,
we can feel God's presence. We don't need to physically see
God to know that He exists and that He's working.

*You are like the wind, Lord. Powerful and fast-moving,
soft and gentle. We may not see You, but we can sense You.
Help us to believe even when we can't see. Amen.*

Loving the Unlovable

"You have heard the law that says, 'Love your neighbor' and hate your enemy. But I say, love your enemies! Pray for those who persecute you! In that way, you will be acting as true children of your Father in heaven."

MATTHEW 5:43-45 NLT

Sometimes running into difficult people can actually be "divine appointments"! Maybe you're the only person they'll see all week who wears a smile. When you happen upon difficult people whom you'd rather not talk to, take the time to pray for your attitude, and then pray for those people. Greet them with a smile and look them in the eye. There is no reason to fear difficult people if you trust in God. He will show you what to do and say as you listen to His promptings (Luke 12:12).

Heavenly Father, I pray that You would help me not to shy away from the people You have allowed to cross my path. Help me speak Your truth and share Your love boldly.

Standing in the Light

Though I have fallen, I will rise.
Though I sit in darkness, the LORD will be my light.
MICAH 7:8 NIV

We may fall down, but God will lift us up. We may feel surrounded by darkness on every side, but He will be our light, guiding the way, showing us which step to take next. No matter where we are, what we've done, or what we're facing, God is our Rescuer, our Savior, and our Friend.

Satan wants to convince us that we have no hope, no future. But God's children always have a future and a hope. We are cherished, and we belong to Him.

Dear Father, thank You for giving me confidence in a future filled with good things. When I'm down, remind me to trust in Your love. Thank You for lifting me out of darkness to stand in Your light.

Praying the Mind of Christ

*We demolish arguments and every pretension that sets
itself up against the knowledge of God, and we take
captive every thought to make it obedient to Christ.*

2 CORINTHIANS 10:5 NIV

By reading and praying scripture and using positive
statements in our prayers that claim what God has already
said He will do for us, the mind of Christ is being activated
in us. By taking captive every thought, we learn to know what
thoughts are of God, what thoughts belong to us, and what
thoughts are of the enemy. Recognize, take captive, and bind
up the thoughts that are of the enemy, and throw them out!
The more we commune with God, fellowship with Him, and
learn from Him, the more we cultivate the mind of Christ.

*Lord, help me identify the thoughts that are not Your
thoughts. Help me purge them. In this way, I will hear You
more clearly so I may be an obedient disciple. Amen!*

Refreshment in Dry Times

The grass withers and the flowers fall,
but the word of our God stands forever.

ISAIAH 40:8 NIV

Sometimes our lives feel just like the grass—dry and listless.
Maybe we're in a season where things seem to stand still:
we've tried everything to change our circumstances for the
better, but to no avail. It is during those times that we need
to remember the faithfulness of God and the permanence
of His Word. His promises to us are many and true! God
will never leave us or forsake us; and He will provide for,
love, and protect us. And—just like the drought—eventually
our personal dry times will give way to times of growth,
refreshment, and beauty.

Dear Lord, help me to remember Your love during difficult
times of dryness. You are everything I need and the
refreshment I seek. Praises to my Living Water!

The End of Your Rope

Do not be far from me,
for trouble is near and there is no one to help.

PSALM 22:11 NIV

Jesus reaches down and wraps you in His loving arms when you call to Him for help. The Bible tells us that He is close to the brokenhearted (Psalm 34:18). We may not have the answers we are looking for here in this life, but we can be sure of this: God sees our pain and loves us desperately. Call to Him in times of trouble. If you feel that you're at the end of your rope, look up! His mighty hand is reaching toward you.

Heavenly Father, I feel alone and afraid.
Surround me with Your love and give me peace and joy.

Jungle of Life

*God's word is alive and working and is sharper than a
double-edged sword. It cuts all the way into us, where the
soul and the spirit are joined, to the center of our joints and
bones. And it judges the thoughts and feelings in our hearts.*

HEBREWS 4:12 NCV

When you take the Bible and live according to His plans,
obeying Him, God's Word cuts like a machete through the
entanglements of life. When you choose to use the Sword
of Truth, it clears a path and can free you from the weights
of the world that try to entrap and ensnare you. No matter
what the challenges of life are saying to you today, take His
Word and speak His plans into your life. Choose His words of
encouragement and peace instead of the negative things life's
circumstances are telling you.

*God, I want to live in Your Truth. I want to believe what You
say about me in the Bible. Help me to speak Your words
today instead of my problems. Help me believe.*

O the Deep, Deep Love of Jesus

*I pray that out of his glorious riches he may strengthen you
with power through his Spirit in your inner being, so that
Christ may dwell in your hearts through faith. And I pray
that you, being rooted and established in love, may have
power, together with all the Lord's holy people, to grasp how
wide and long and high and deep is the love of Christ.*

EPHESIANS 3:16–18 NIV

What an amazing picture. That God should care for us in such
a way is almost incomprehensible. Despite our shortcomings,
our sin, He loves us. It takes a measure of faith to believe in
His love. When we feel a nagging thought of unworthiness,
of being unlovable, trust in the Word and sing a new song.
For His love is deep and wide.

---

*Lord, thank You for loving me
even when I'm unlovable. Amen.*

The Ultimate Act of Love

Bring joy to your servant, Lord, for I put my trust
in you. You, Lord, are forgiving and good,
abounding in love to all who call to you.

PSALM 86:4–5 NIV

Forgiveness doesn't require that the people who did the hurting apologize or acknowledge what they've done. It's not about making the score even. It doesn't even require forgetting about the incident. But it is about admitting that the one who hurt us is human, just like we are. We surrender our right for revenge and, like God, let go and give the wrongdoer mercy, therefore blessing them.

Gracious and loving Father, thank You that You love me
and have forgiven me of my sins. May I be more like
You in forgiving others. Although I may not be able to
forgive as easily as You do, please encourage me to
take those small steps. In forgiving others, Father,
I am that much closer to being like You. Amen.

I Grow Weary

But those who wait for the Lord [who expect, look for, and hope in Him] shall change and renew their strength and power; they shall lift their wings and mount up [close to God] as eagles [mount up to the sun]; they shall run and not be weary, they shall walk and not faint or become tired.

ISAIAH 40:31 AMPC

As long as we are warring inside, we will not find rest. We must find out what Jesus wants for our lives and then obey. Feasting on His Word and learning more about Him will give us the direction we need and the ability to trust. It is only when we understand our salvation and surrender that we can come to Him, unencumbered by guilt or fear, and lay our head on His chest. Safe within His embrace, we can rest. We will be as a well-watered garden, refreshed and blessed by our loving Creator.

Father, I am weary and need Your refreshing Spirit to guide me. I trust in You. Amen.

Reap in Joy!

Remember this: Whoever sows sparingly
will also reap sparingly, and whoever sows
generously will also reap generously.

2 CORINTHIANS 9:6 NIV

Each of us wants to feel appreciated, and we like to deal with a friendly person. Have you ever worked with a person who seemed to have a perpetually bad attitude? You probably didn't feel particularly encouraged after an encounter with this coworker. Yes, sometimes things go wrong, but your attitude in the thick of it is determined by your expectations. If you expect things to turn out well, you'll generally have a positive mental attitude. Treat everyone with genuine kindness, courtesy, and respect, and that is what will be reflected back to you.

Heavenly Father, help me plant the seeds of patience,
love, compassion, and courtesy in all those I come in
contact with. Please let me make an eternal difference
in these people's lives. I want to joyfully reap
a rich harvest for Your Kingdom. Amen!

Why Praise God?

Though he slay me, yet will I trust in him.
JOB 13:15 KJV

It's difficult to praise God when problems press in harder than a crowd exiting a burning building. But that's the time to praise Him the most. We wait for our circumstances to change, yet God desires to change us despite them. Praise coupled with prayer in our darkest moments is what moves the mighty hand of God to work in our hearts and lives. How can we pray and praise God when everything goes wrong? The bigger question might be: How can we not?

---

*Jesus, help me to pray and praise You
despite my circumstances.*

Everlasting Light

In him was life, and that life was the light of all
mankind. The light shines in the darkness,
and the darkness has not overcome it.

JOHN 1:4–5 NIV

Focus on the fact that Jesus is the Light of the World who holds out wonderful hope for us. Set your prayer life to start with praise and adoration of the King of kings. Lift your voice in song or read out loud from the Word. The Light will eliminate the darkness every time. Keep your heart and mind set on Him as you walk through the day. Praise Him for every little thing; nothing is too small for God. A grateful heart and constant praise will bring the Light into your day.

Dear Lord, how we love You. We trust in You this day
to lead us on the right path lit with Your Light. Amen.

The Word for Every Day

As for God, his way is perfect; the word of the LORD
is tried: he is a buckler to all them that trust in him.

2 SAMUEL 22:31 KJV

God's Word is such an incredible gift, one that goes hand in
hand with prayer. It's amazing, really, that the Creator of the
Universe gave us the scriptures as His personal Word to us.
When we're faithful to pick up the Word, He is faithful to use it
to encourage us. Reading and praying through scripture is one
of the keys to finding and keeping our sanity, peace, and joy.

God, thank You for Your gift of the holy scriptures
and for sweet communion with You through prayer.

The Right Focus

*Turning your ear to wisdom and applying your heart
to understanding—indeed, if you call out for insight
and cry aloud for understanding, and if you look for it
as for silver and search for it as for hidden treasure,
then you will understand the fear of the LORD
and find the knowledge of God.*

PROVERBS 2:2–5 NIV

Frustration and stress can keep us from clearly seeing the
things that God puts before us. Time spent in prayer and
meditation on God's Word can often wash away the dirt and
grime of the day-to-day and provide a clear picture of God's
intentions for our lives. Step outside the pressure and into
His presence and get the right focus for whatever you're
facing today.

*Lord, help me to avoid distractions
and keep my eyes on You.*

Pass It On!

*After the usual readings from the books of Moses
and the prophets, those in charge of the service sent
them this message: "Brothers, if you have any word
of encouragement for the people, come and give it."*

ACTS 13:15 NLT

Encouragement brings hope. Have you ever received a
word from someone that instantly lifted your spirit? Did
you receive a bit of good news or something that diminished
your negative outlook? Perhaps a particular conversation
helped to bring your problems into perspective. Paul passed
on encouragement, and many benefited. So the next time
you're encouraged, pass it on! You may never know how your
words or actions benefited someone else.

*Lord, thank You for the wellspring of
encouragement through Your holy Word.*

Seek God

I love all who love me.
Those who search will surely find me.

PROVERBS 8:17 NLT

Scripture tells us that God loves those who love Him and that if we search for Him, we will surely find Him. One translation of the Bible says it this way: "Those who seek me early and diligently will find me." Seek God in all things and in all ways. Search for Him in each moment of every day you are blessed to walk on this earth. He is found easily in His creation and in His Word. He is with you. Just look for Him. He wants to be found!

Father in Heaven, thank You for Your unfailing
love for me. Help me to search for You diligently.
I know that when I seek You I will find You. Amen.

When You Give Your Life Away

Which of you, intending to build a tower,
sitteth not down first, and counteth the cost,
whether he have sufficient to finish it?

LUKE 14:28 KJV

Every person has the same amount of life each day. What matters is how you spend it. It's easy to waste your day doing insignificant things, leaving little time for God. The most important things in life are eternal endeavors: Spending time in prayer to God for others. Giving your life to building a relationship with God by reading His Word and growing in faith. Sharing Christ with others and giving them the opportunity to know Him. These are things that will last. What are you spending your life on? What are you getting out of what you give yourself to each day?

Heavenly Father, my life is full. I ask that You give me
wisdom and instruction to give my life to the things
that matter most. The time I have is precious and
valuable. Help me to invest it wisely in eternal things.

121

Thankful, Thankful Heart

I will praise you, Lord, with all my heart.
I will tell all the miracles you have done.

PSALM 9:1 NCV

When you choose to approach life from the positive side, you can find thankfulness in most of life's circumstances. It completely changes your outlook, your attitude, and your countenance. When you are tempted to feel sorry for yourself or to blame others or God for difficulties, push PAUSE. Take a moment and rewind your life. Look back and count the blessings God has given you. As you remind yourself of all He has done for you and in you, it will bring change to your attitude and give you hope in the situation you're facing. Count your blessings today.

Lord, I am thankful for my life and all You have done for me.
When life happens, help me to respond to it in a healthy,
positive way. Remind me to look to You and trust
You to carry me through life's challenges.

Love Your Enemies

Love your enemies, do good to them, and lend to
them without expecting to get anything back.
Then your reward will be great.

LUKE 6:35 NIV

God calls us to a love so brave, so intense that it defies logic and turns the world on its side. He calls us to love like He loves. That means we must show patience where others have been short. We must show kindness where others have been cruel. We must look for ways to bless when others have cursed. God promises great rewards for those who do this. Oh, the rewards may not be immediate. But when God promises great rewards, we can know without doubt that any present struggle will be repaid with goodness and blessing many times over.

Dear Father, help me to love those who hate me,
bless those who curse me, and show kindness to those
who have been cruel to me. Help me to love like You love.

Rejoice!

Rejoice in the Lord always.
I will say it again: Rejoice!

PHILIPPIANS 4:4 NIV

When God is the source of our joy, we will never lose that joy. Circumstances may frustrate us and break our hearts. But God is able to supply all our needs. He is able to restore broken relationships. He can give us new jobs or help us to succeed at our current jobs. Through it all—despite it all—we can rejoice in knowing that we are God's and that He loves us.

Dear Father, thank You for loving me.
Help me to make You the source of my joy.

Unshakeable Love

"For even if the mountains walk away and the hills
fall to pieces, My love won't walk away from you,
my covenant commitment of peace won't fall apart."
The GOD who has compassion on you says so.

ISAIAH 54:10 MSG

We must rest in God's wild, unbending love for us. He promises
in Isaiah that no matter what happens, He will never remove
Himself from us. When we believe Him wholeheartedly and
rest in His love, we will be filled with fear-busting peace and
adventurous faith. That faith allows us to dream big dreams
and conquer the worries that keep us chained.

Lord, thank You for Your love, which never leaves me.
Help me to rest in Your love above all else.

Unfailing Love

I will instruct you and teach you in the way you should go; I will counsel you with my loving eye on you. Many are the woes of the wicked, but the LORD's unfailing love surrounds the one who trusts in him.

PSALM 32:8, 10 NIV

God's love surrounds us always—if we trust in Him. Have you put your complete trust in the Lord? If not, open your heart to Him and ask Him to become the Lord of your life. Jesus is standing at the door of your heart, ready to come in when you respond (Revelation 3:20). Or maybe you've already accepted Christ as your Savior, but you're not really sure if He can be trusted. Know that He has been faithful to His children through all generations and that He is working out every circumstance in your life for your own good (Romans 8:28).

Father God, I praise You for Your unfailing love.
Continue to counsel me and lead me in the way
I should go. Thank You for watching over me.

Look Up!

Your love, LORD, reaches to the heavens,
your faithfulness to the skies.

PSALM 36:5 NIV

In Bible times, people often studied the sky. Looking up at the heavens reminded them of God and His mighty wonders. A rainbow was God's sign to Noah that a flood would never again destroy the earth. God used a myriad of stars to foretell Abraham's abundant family, and a single star heralded Christ's birth. This immense space that we call "sky" is a reflection of God's infinite love and faithfulness. So take time today. Look up at the heavens and thank God for His endless love.

Heavenly Father, remind me to stop and appreciate
Your wonderful creations. And as I look upward,
fill me with Your infinite love. Amen.

Thou Shalt Not Worry!

Do not worry about tomorrow, for tomorrow will worry about itself. Each day has enough trouble of its own.

MATTHEW 6:34 NIV

What if the Lord had written an eleventh commandment, "Thou shalt not worry"? In a sense, He did! He commands us in various scriptures not to fret. So cast your anxieties on the Lord. Give them up! Let them go! Don't let worries zap your strength and your joy. Today is a gift from the Lord. Don't sacrifice it to fears and frustrations! Let them go. . .and watch God work!

Father God, lift all anxiety from my heart, and make my spirit light again. I know that I can't do it on my own. But with You, I can let go. . .and watch You work! I praise You, God!

Joy. . .Minute by Minute

Keep your eyes focused on what is right,
and look straight ahead to what is good.
PROVERBS 4:25 NCV

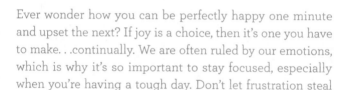

Ever wonder how you can be perfectly happy one minute and upset the next? If joy is a choice, then it's one you have to make. . .continually. We are often ruled by our emotions, which is why it's so important to stay focused, especially when you're having a tough day. Don't let frustration steal even sixty seconds from you. Instead, choose joy!

Dear heavenly Father, please help me to keep my
emotions in check today—and every day. If I keep
my focus on You. . .and Your goodness,
God, I can always choose joy.

An Offering of Joy

*Then my head will be exalted above the enemies who
surround me; at his sacred tent I will sacrifice with
shouts of joy; I will sing and make music to the Lord.*

PSALM 27:6 NIV

It's one thing to offer a sacrifice of joy when things are
going your way and people are treating you fairly. But when
you've been through a terrible betrayal, it's often hard to
recapture that feeling of joy. As you encounter hurts and
betrayals, remember that God is the lifter of your head.
Sing praises and continue to offer a sacrifice of joy!

*Lord, lift my head. Wrap me in Your warm embrace.
Help me to remember that even though I've experienced
betrayal, I can still praise You and offer a
sacrifice of joy. I love You, Father!*

A Joyous Treasure

The kingdom of heaven is like treasure hidden in a field.
When a man found it, he hid it again, and then in his joy
went and sold all he had and bought that field.

MATTHEW 13:44 NIV

Have you ever stumbled across a rare treasure, one so priceless that you were willing to trade everything you owned to have it? If you've given your heart to Christ, if you've accepted His work on Calvary, then you have already obtained the greatest treasure of all. . .new life in Him. Oh, what immeasurable joy comes from knowing He's placed that treasure in your heart for all eternity!

Father, thank You for the gift of Your Son.
Because of Your loving sacrifice, I can forever
have joy in my heart, knowing that I will
spend eternity in heaven with You.

Joy in the Battle

Then they returned, every man of Judah and Jerusalem,
and Jehoshaphat in the forefront of them, to go again
to Jerusalem with joy; for the LORD had made
them to rejoice over their enemies.

2 CHRONICLES 20:27 KJV

Enemy forces were just around the bend. Jehoshaphat, king of Judah, called his people together. After much prayer, he sent the worshippers (the Levites) to the front lines, singing joyful praises as they went. The battle was won! When you face your next battle, praise your way through it! Strength and joy will rise up within you! Prepare for victory!

No matter what kind of hardship I face, Father God,
I want to praise my way through it and come through
even stronger than I was before. Thank You for helping
me to win life's battles, both large and small.

Eternal Joy!

*And the ransomed of the LORD shall return, and come to
Zion with songs and everlasting joy upon their heads:
they shall obtain joy and gladness, and sorrow
and sighing shall flee away.*

ISAIAH 35:10 KJV

Have you ever pondered eternity? Forever and ever and
ever. . . ? Our finite minds can't grasp the concept, and yet
there is one thing we understand from scripture—we will
enter eternity in a state of everlasting joy and gladness. No
more tears! No sorrow! An eternal joy-fest awaits us! Now
that's something to celebrate!

*When life becomes difficult, help me to keep things in
perspective, Father. The hardships I face in the day-to-
day are but blips in time compared to the eternal joy I will
experience in heaven. Thank You for joy that lasts forever.*

Joyous Freedom

Blessed is he whose transgression is forgiven,
whose sin is covered.

PSALM 32:1 KJV

What if you were locked up in a prison cell for years on end? You wait for the day when the jailer turns that key in the lock, releasing you once and for all. In a sense, experiencing God's forgiveness is like being set free from prison. Can you fathom the joy? Walking into the sunshine for the first time in years? Oh, praise Him for His forgiveness today!

Sweet freedom, Lord. . . It's a beautiful feeling to have experienced the joy of Your complete and utter forgiveness. Thank You for setting my spirit free!

Pressed Down, Running Over

Give, and it shall be given unto you; good measure,
pressed down, and shaken together, and running over,
shall men give into your bosom.

LUKE 6:38 KJV

"Give, and it shall be given unto you." If you've been walking with the Lord for any length of time, you've likely heard this dozens of times. Do we give so that we can get? No, we give out of a grateful heart, and the Lord—in His generosity—meets our needs. Today, pause and thank Him for the many gifts He has given you. Do you feel the joy running over?

Lord, help me to always give from a grateful heart
and never because I plan to get something in return.
You have given me abundant blessings, Father.
Thank You for always meeting my needs.

Who Exalts?

*No one from the east or the west or from the desert
can exalt themselves. It is God who judges:
he brings one down, he exalts another.*

PSALM 75:6-7 NIV

Sometimes we grumble when others are exalted. We feel left out. Why do others prosper when everything around us seems to be falling apart? We can't celebrate their victories. We aren't joyful for them. Shame on us! God chooses who to exalt. . .and when to do so. We can't pretend to know His thoughts. But we can submit to His will and celebrate with those who are walking through seasons of great favor.

---

*God, it's so hard to be happy for others when I feel like
I haven't been blessed in the same way. Please help me
to rejoice when others experience Your favor.
I will continue to trust that You have a plan
for my life—and that Your plan is good!*

A Sacrifice of Praise

Is any among you afflicted? let him pray.
Is any merry? let him sing psalms.
JAMES 5:13 KJV

It's tough to praise when you're not feeling well, isn't it? But that's exactly what God calls us to do. If you're struggling today, reach way down deep. . . Out of your pain, your weakness, offer God a sacrifice of praise. Spend serious time in prayer. Lift up a song of joy, even if it's a weak song! You'll be surprised how He energizes you with His great joy!

I'm struggling today, God. But that's no surprise to You, is it? You know just how I feel. Please energize my sluggish spirit. I want to sing praises to You!

Joyful in Glory

Let the saints be joyful in glory:
let them sing aloud upon their beds.

PSALM 149:5 KJV

When do you like to spend time alone with the Lord? In the morning, as the stillness of the day sweeps over you? At night, when you rest your head upon the pillow? Start your conversation with praise. Let your favorite worship song or hymn pour forth! Tell Him how blessed you are to be His child. This private praise time will strengthen you and will fill your heart with joy!

As I enter into this conversation with You, Father,
I praise You. Thank You for being
Lord—and leader—of my life.

Finishing with Joy

*But none of these things move me, neither count I
my life dear unto myself, so that I might
finish my course with joy.*

ACTS 20:24 KJV

The Christian life is a journey, isn't it? We move from point A to point B and then on from there, all the while growing in our faith. Instead of focusing on the ups and downs of the journey, we should be looking ahead to the finish line. We want to be people who finish well. Today, set your sights on that unseen line that lies ahead. What joy will come when you cross it!

---

*Father God, help me to keep my eyes on the finish line
so I can finish my journey with joy.*

Everyday Joy

For in him we live, and move,
and have our being.

ACTS 17:28 KJV

Every breath we breathe comes from God. Every step we take is a gift from our Creator. We can do nothing apart from Him. In the same sense, every joy, every sorrow. . .God goes through each one with us. His heart is for us. We can experience joy in our everyday lives, even when things aren't going our way. We simply have to remember that He is in control. We have our being. . .in Him!

Thank You for being in control of all things, God.
I would rather have You by my side than anyone
else in the world—through every up, down,
and in between, You are there!

Mercy Multiplied

Mercy unto you, and peace,
and love, be multiplied.
JUDE 1:2 KJV

Have you ever done the math on God's mercy? If so, you've probably figured out that it just keeps multiplying itself out over and over again. We mess up; He extends mercy. We mess up again; He pours out mercy once again. In the same way, peace, love, and joy are multiplied back to us. Praise the Lord! God's mathematics work in our favor.

Father God, I am so thankful that Your
math works differently than mine!

Go Out with Joy

For ye shall go out with joy, and be led forth with peace:
the mountains and the hills shall break forth
before you into singing, and all the trees
of the field shall clap their hands.

ISAIAH 55:12 KJV

God reveals Himself in a million different ways, but perhaps the most breathtaking is through nature. The next time you're in a mountainous spot, pause and listen. Can you hear the sound of God's eternal song? Does joy radiate through your being? Aren't you filled with wonder and with peace? The Lord has, through the beauty of nature, given us a rare and glorious gift.

When I view the wonders of Your marvelous creation,
Lord, my heart fills with absolute joy!

Second Chances

For his anger lasts only a moment, but his favor
lasts a lifetime; weeping may stay for the night,
but rejoicing comes in the morning.

PSALM 30:5 NIV

Don't you love second chances? New beginnings? If only we could go back and redo some of our past mistakes. . . What better choices we'd make the second time around. Life in Jesus is all about the rebirth experience—the opportunity to start over. Each day is a new day, in fact. And praise God! The sorrows and trials of yesterday are behind us. With each new morning, joy dawns!

I am so glad You allow second chances, Father.
Thank You for each new morning that
is an opportunity to start over!

Joyous Tomorrow

But if we hope for that we see not,
then do we with patience wait for it.

ROMANS 8:25 KJV

Are you in a "waiting" season? Is your patience being tested to the breaking point? Take heart! You are not alone. Every godly man and woman from biblical times till now went through seasons of waiting on the Lord. Their secret? They hoped for what they could not see. (They never lost their hope!) And they waited patiently. So as you're waiting, reflect on the biblical giants and realize. . .you're not alone!

Father, thank You for Your Word, which gives examples
of others who have walked the same path before me.
Because of You, I know that I am not alone—
today, tomorrow, or any day after that!

Enjoying Life

Let all who seek You rejoice and be glad in You; and let those who love Your salvation say continually, "Let God be magnified."...You are my help and my deliverer.

PSALM 70:4–5 NASB

Sometimes we approach God robotically: "Lord, please do this for me. Lord, please do that." We're convinced we'll be happy, if only God grants our wishes—like a genie in a bottle. We're going about this backward! We should start by praising God. Thank Him for life, health, and many answered prayers. Our joyous praise will remind us just how blessed we already are! Then, out of genuine relationship, we make our requests known.

Father God, my joy comes from You—and only You. Without You I could never experience all of the joys that life has to offer. Thank You!

A Royal Vision

Yes, joyful are those who live like this!
Joyful indeed are those whose God is the LORD.

PSALM 144:15 NLT

How wonderful to realize you're God's child. He loves you and wants nothing but good for you. Doesn't knowing you're His daughter send waves of joy through your soul? How happy we are when we recognize that we are princesses. . .children of the most high God! Listen closely as He whispers royal secrets in your ear. Your heavenly Father offers you keys to the Kingdom. . .and vision for the road ahead.

Joy floods my soul when I think about how much You love me, Lord. Thank You for making me Your child.

The Key to Happiness

He who heeds the word wisely will find good,
*and whoever trusts in the L*ORD*, happy is he.*

PROVERBS 16:20 NKJV

Want the key to true happiness? Try wisdom. When others around you are losing their heads, losing their cool, and losing sleep over their decisions, choose to react differently. Step up to the plate. Handle matters wisely. Wise choices always lead to joyous outcomes. And along the way, you will be setting an example for others around you to follow. So, c'mon. . .get happy! Get wisdom!

Father, thank You for the wisdom of Your Word,
which will always point me in the right
direction when I have a choice to make.

A Net of Love

No one has ever seen God; but if we love one another,
God lives in us and his love is made complete in us.

1 JOHN 4:12 NIV

It's hard to be a good witness if you've got a sour expression on your face. People aren't usually won to the Lord by grumpy friends and coworkers. If you hope to persuade people that life in Jesus is the ultimate experience, then you've got to let your enthusiasm shine through. Before you reach for the net, spend some time on your knees, asking for an infusion of joy. Then go catch some fish!

Dear heavenly Father, I want to be a good witness
for You. Help me remember to exude joy and
love—so others will be drawn to You.

Not Withholding

Anything I wanted, I would take. I denied myself no pleasure. I even found great pleasure in hard work, a reward for all my labors.

ECCLESIASTES 2:10 NLT

Work beckons. Deadlines loom. You're trying to balance your home life against your work life, and it's overwhelming. Take heart! It is possible to rejoice in your labors, to find pleasure in the day-to-day tasks. At work or at play. . .let the Lord cause a song of joy to rise up in your heart.

Help me to slow down—every day—and enjoy the moments as they come, Father God. May I not become so busy that I miss out on life's simple pleasures.

Joy in Your Work

Go, eat your food with gladness, and drink your wine with a joyful heart, for God has already approved what you do.

ECCLESIASTES 9:7 NIV

Ever feel like nothing you do is good enough? Your boss is frustrated over something you've done wrong. The kids are complaining. Your neighbors are even upset at you. How wonderful to read that God accepts our work, even when we feel lacking. He encourages us to go our way with a merry heart, completely confident that we are accepted in the Beloved.

When it feels like I'm a complete failure—and that I am letting others down, Lord—please infuse my soul with confidence. No matter what, I am Yours. I am accepted. I am loved.

He First Loved Us

This is how God showed his love among us:
He sent his one and only Son into the world
that we might live through him.

1 JOHN 4:9 NIV

Many things about God are quite a mystery. If there is anything at all that we can understand for sure, though, we can know He loves us. There is nothing we could ever do to make God *stop* loving us, because certainly we did nothing to make Him start. God is concerned about everything we do. He celebrates our victories and cries with us during our difficult times. God proved His love for us long before we were ever born! How could we not love such a God, who first loved us so much?

You have always loved me, God, and You will love me forever. I am so grateful! Compared to Yours, my love is small, but I love You with all of my heart. Amen.

Soul Comfort

In the multitude of my anxieties within me,
your comforts delight my soul.

PSALM 94:19 NKJV

We don't know for sure who wrote Psalm 94, but we can be certain that the psalmist was annoyed and anxious when he wrote it. He cries out to God, asking Him to "pay back to the proud what they deserve" (v. 2 NIV). Then he goes on with a list of accusations about the evil ones... "In the multitude of my anxieties within me." Does that phrase describe you? When anxiety overwhelms us, we find relief in the words of Psalm 94:19. When we turn our anxious thoughts over to God, He brings contentment to our souls.

Dear God, on those days when frustration and anxiety
overwhelm me, please come to me, comfort my soul,
and remind me to praise You. Amen.

Shine On!

Let the message about Christ, in all its richness,
fill your lives. Teach and counsel each other with all
the wisdom he gives. Sing psalms and hymns and
spiritual songs to God with thankful hearts.

COLOSSIANS 3:16 NLT

We need to live the Word of God every day. It will shine through us! The old song says, "They will know we are Christians by our love." This means reflecting the love of God in everything we do. When we spend time in God's Word, we find peace, wisdom, and contentment that we get from no other place. This is a peace we love to have. This is happiness! Imagine being anything but thankful to God for filling us with His love, peace, and wisdom!

O Lord, my Rock and my Redeemer, may my words
and my actions be a reflection of Your Word
and pleasing in Your sight. Amen.

Visible Reminders

Let the morning bring me word of your unfailing love,
for I have put my trust in you.

PSALM 143:8 NIV

We don't know if David was a morning person or a night owl, but he chose to start his day looking for visible reminders of God's unfailing love. It might have been easy to remember God's love for him if he had witnessed a glorious morning sunrise, but if the night had been stormy and he was dealing with spooked sheep in the midst of a downpour, God's unfailing love may have felt a little distant. Whether or not conditions were favorable for faith, David believed in God's unfailing love—even if he couldn't see it in the world around him.

I awake in the morning, and You are there. You are
with me all day long and throughout the night. Thank You,
heavenly Father, for Your ever-present love. Amen.

Loyal Hearts

For the eyes of the Lord range throughout the earth to strengthen those whose hearts are fully committed to him.

2 Chronicles 16:9 niv

God seeks a relationship with those who have open and receiving hearts. He is not looking to condemn or judge but to find hearts committed to knowing Him and learning His way. He desires people who want to talk and listen to Him and who have a deep thirst to serve and please Him. God looks for us, and the only requirement is for each of us to have a fully devoted heart. We open our hearts and hands to receive Him, and He will find us.

Find me, Lord; draw me near to You. Open up my heart so that I may fully receive all that You want to pour into it. Amen.

God's Command

So He said, "Come." And when Peter had come down out
of the boat, he walked on the water to go to Jesus.

MATTHEW 14:29 NKJV

Jesus stayed behind to send the crowds away—and then to
pray. Later that evening, the disciples, wrestling their boat
against a contrary wind, saw a ghostly figure approaching.
Jesus assured them it was He, and Peter asked the Lord to
command him to come. Jesus did—and Peter, briefly, walked
on water. What does it take for an ordinary person to walk on
water? A command of God. By the power of God, ordinary
men and women, responding to God's call, have successfully
accomplished difficult, even impossible, tasks.

You are my strength, O Lord. Whenever I feel like giving up,
I will turn to You, believing that You will give me
the power to carry on. Amen.

God of Possible

*Jesus looked at them and said, "With man this is
impossible, but with God all things are possible."*

MATTHEW 19:26 NIV

No one can be saved by their own efforts! Man's greatest
efforts pale in comparison to the requirements of a holy God.
But grace, freely offered by God and accepted by individuals,
will admit us to heaven. With God, all things *are* possible—
even enabling forgiven sinners to live eternally. Realizing we
can do nothing is the key to gaining everything.

*Dear Father, I appreciate Your grace, Your lovingkindness
that I don't deserve. There is nothing I have done to earn it.
Grace is Your gift to me, and I thank You. Amen.*

Every Step of the Way

Never stop praying.

1 THESSALONIANS 5:17 NLT

God wants to be involved in our daily routines. He wants to hear from us, and He waits for us. God never promised an easy life to Christians. If we will allow Him, though, God will be there with us every step of the way. All we need to do is to come to Him in prayer. With these three simple words from 1 Thessalonians 5:17, our lives can be fulfilling as we live to communicate with our Lord.

Father, when I pray, remind me that prayer is not only about talking to You but also about listening to You. Open my heart to Your words. Amen.

Planted Deep

Fix these words of mine in your hearts and minds;
tie them as symbols on your hands and
bind them on your foreheads.

DEUTERONOMY 11:18 NIV

Memorizing Bible verses isn't a fashionable trend in today's world, but learning key verses plants the Word of God deeply in our hearts. We draw strength and nourishment in dark times from remembering what God told us in the Bible. In times of crisis we recall God's promises of hope and comfort. In our everyday moments, repeating well-known verses reminds us that God is always with us—whether we feel like it or not.

What an awesome gift You have given me, God—
the Bible! I will fix Your words in my mind and heart
and carry them with me wherever I go. Amen.

Revel in the Beauty

He has made everything beautiful in its time.
He has also set eternity in the human heart; yet no one
can fathom what God has done from beginning to end.
ECCLESIASTES 3:11 NIV

No one can completely "fathom what God has done." That's what makes Him God. And yet, still we try. Thankfully, our hearts don't need to understand; neither do they need earthly "fixes." They just need to be set free, to find God and revel in the beauty of His never-ending creation. Believers, stop letting unanswerable questions prevent you from loving Him more completely. And unbelievers, ask yourself, if you had every material thing you could want, wouldn't your heart still be reaching out for eternity?

I have questions, God, so many unanswered questions
about life and about You. Increase my trust in You.
Help me to set aside my uncertainty and
delight in Your never-ending love. Amen.

Keep Smiling

When they were discouraged, I smiled and that
encouraged them, and lightened their spirits.

JOB 29:24 TLB

Our most authentic forms of communication occur without
a word. Rather, they flow from an understanding smile, a
compassionate touch, a loving gesture, a gentle presence,
or an unspoken prayer. God used Job, an ordinary man with
an extraordinary amount of love and wisdom—a man whose
only adornment was righteous living and a warm smile. And
He wants to use us, too. So keep smiling. Someone may just
need it.

Remind me, Jesus, to bless others through my actions.
A warm smile, a simple act of kindness, or a loving touch
might be just what someone needs today. Amen.

Love Is. . .

And now these three remain: faith,
hope and love. But the greatest of these is love.

1 CORINTHIANS 13:13 NIV

Who can deny the power of faith? Throughout history, faith has closed the mouths of lions, opened blinded eyes, and saved countless lost souls. And the scriptures note that without it we cannot please God (Hebrews 11:6). Yet as wonderful as these qualities are, it is love that God deems the greatest. Love lasts and never fails. It is patient, kind, unselfish, and honest; it never keeps a record of wrongs or delights in evil. In a word, love is God. And there is no *One* greater.

Father, I strive to love patiently, kindly, unselfishly,
and honestly because in doing so I become more
perfect in love and more like You! Amen.

God's Heart

I will give them an undivided heart and put a new spirit
in them; I will remove from them their heart of stone
and give them a heart of flesh.

EZEKIEL 11:19 NIV

God is willing to give us an undivided heart—a heart that
is open and ready to see, hear, and love. This heart has a
single focus: loving God and others with a tenderness that
we know comes from Someone beyond us. The good news
is we have already had successful surgery, and our donor
hearts are within us. We received our heart transplants
when Jesus died for us, creating new spirits within us. God's
heart changes everything and makes us into new people
with living hearts.

Thank You, Lord, for giving me a new heart, a heart so
perfect in love that it will last me forever. Amen.

Never Alone

But the Advocate, the Holy Spirit, whom the Father
will send in my name, will teach you all things and will
remind you of everything I have said to you.

JOHN 14:26 NIV

Jesus called the Holy Spirit "the Advocate," a translation of
the Greek word *parakletos*: "one called alongside to help." It
can also indicate Strengthener, Comforter, Helper, Adviser,
Counselor, Intercessor, Ally, and Friend. The Holy Spirit
walks with us to help, instruct, comfort, and accomplish God's
work on earth. Through His presence inside us, we know the
Father. In our deepest time of need, He is there. He comforts
and reveals to us the truth of God's Word. Jesus is always with
us because His Spirit lives in our hearts.

Strengthener, Comforter, Helper, Adviser, Counselor,
Intercessor, Ally, Friend—oh, Holy Spirit of God!
Thank You for dwelling within my heart, guiding me
and drawing me near to the Father. Amen.

God-Breathed

All Scripture is inspired by God and is useful to teach us
what is true and to make us realize what is wrong
in our lives. It corrects us when we are wrong
and teaches us to do what is right.

2 TIMOTHY 3:16 NLT

God's Word continues to be God-breathed! It is as relevant today as it ever was! Scripture speaks to us in our current situations just as it did to people a few thousand years ago. . .just as it will for eternity. Situations and cultures and languages and technologies have changed all throughout history, but God has been able to speak to people exactly where they are through His living Word. There is certainly no other book nor collection of books in the world that can do that—only the living Word, which continues to be God-breathed.

Dear God, all things pass into history except for You and Your Word. How wonderful it is that Your Word transcends time, is relevant in the present, and will live forever! Amen.

Joyful Service

Wherefore I put thee in remembrance
that thou stir up the gift of God, which is in thee.

2 TIMOTHY 1:6 KJV

This passage is a reminder to every believer. It demonstrates that our God-given gifts remain strong only through active use and fostering. Gifts left unattended or unused become stagnant and, like an unattended fire, die. Just as wood or coal fuels a fire, faith, prayer, and obedience are the fresh fuels of God's grace that keep our fires burning. But this takes action on our part. Are you using the gifts God has given you? Can He entrust you with more? Perhaps today is the day to gather the spiritual tinder necessary to stoke the fire of God within.

God, You have given me special talents and inspiring gifts.
I pray that You would open my eyes to sharing those
gifts. Through faith and obedience I will
joyfully use them to serve You. Amen.

He Hears Me

I love the Lord because he hears
my voice and my prayer for mercy.

PSALM 116:1 NLT

Isn't that mind-blowing? The almighty God of the universe, who created and assembled every particle in existence, hears us when we come before Him. Maybe we go to the Lord in song, praising. Maybe we spend some time reading and thinking about God's Word. Maybe we are praying to Him as we reach out for His comfort. Whatever we do, God hears us and is interested in what we have to say. Isn't that a great reason to love the Lord? May we never forget to give thanks to God daily for the opportunity that He provides for us to simply be heard.

I have so many reasons to love You, Lord, so many reasons
to worship and praise You. How grateful I am that
You hear my voice! I love You, Lord. Amen.

Three in One

I am Alpha and Omega,
the beginning and the end, the first and the last.
REVELATION 22:13 KJV

What makes our God unique among the religions of the world? No other religion has a God whose Son is equal to the Father. Jews and Muslims reject the idea of God having a Son. Only Christianity has a triune God—three persons in one God. The Bible is unique because in it God fully reveals who He is. Since Jesus is fully God, let scripture renew our hope and faith in our Savior. He who created all things out of nothing will re-create this world into a paradise without sin.

Jesus, I learn how to live by Your human example,
and I trust in You as my God—Father, Son, and Holy
Spirit—three persons, one God, one perfect You! Amen.

Endless Supply of Love

We love because he first loved us.

1 JOHN 4:19 NIV

The power of God's love within us fuels our love when human love is running on empty. He plants His love within our hearts so we can share Him with others. We draw from His endless supply. Love starts with God. God continues to provide His love to nourish us. God surrounds us with His love. We live in hope and draw from His strength—all because He first loved us.

Oh God, the human love I know on earth cannot compare with Your love. When I feel empty, Your love fills me up. Your love is perfect. It never fails. Amen.

Never Settle

*For in him dwelleth all the fulness of the Godhead
bodily. And ye are complete in him.*
COLOSSIANS 2:9–10 KJV

Paul stated clearly that the fullness of deity lives in bodily
form in Christ. He is God the Son, and when you have God
in your heart, you are complete. You don't need anything
added—neither ceremonies nor so-called secret knowledge—to
make you *more* complete. If the Spirit of Jesus Christ dwells
in your heart and you are connected to God, you've got it all!
Don't let anyone persuade you otherwise (Colossians 2:8).
Don't settle for substitutes.

*Jesus, You complete me. Since You dwell in my heart,
I am forever connected with God and heaven. I have all that
I need—salvation and Your perfect, eternal love. Amen.*

Extend Hospitality

Do not forget to show hospitality to strangers,
for by so doing some people have shown
hospitality to angels without knowing it.

HEBREWS 13:2 NIV

The author of Hebrews 13:2, most likely Paul, reminded Christians to extend hospitality to strangers. He suggested that some strangers might even be angels sent from God. Today, most strangers to whom we extend generosity and hospitality are probably not angels, but we can't know if someday God will allow us to entertain an angel without us knowing it. When you practice hospitality, God might be using you to minister to others. What are some other ways that you can extend hospitality to strangers?

Lord, teach me to be wise when extending hospitality to
strangers. Enlighten me. Teach me new ways to minister
to others and show them Your amazing love. Amen.

Never Forgotten

See, I have engraved you on the palms of my hands.

ISAIAH 49:16 NIV

In the middle of tumultuous times, it's tempting to proclaim that God has forgotten us. Both Israel and Judah struggled with the idea that God had abandoned them. But God took steps to contradict this notion. In an image that prefigures Jesus' crucifixion, God boldly proclaimed that His children were engraved on the palms of His hands. The nail-scarred hands that His Son would endure bear the engraved names of all of us who call upon Him as Savior and Lord. God does not forget us in the midst of our troubles! It is His nail-scarred hands that reach down and hold our own.

Jesus, the scars on Your hands are because of me—a testament to my salvation. My name is engraved on Your hand as a child of God. Oh thank You, dear Jesus! Amen.

God Knows

Your eyes saw my unformed body; all the days
ordained for me were written in your book
before one of them came to be.

PSALM 139:16 NIV

God knows the days of all people. Job said, "A person's days
are determined; you have decreed the number of his months"
(Job 14:5 NIV). The same knowledge applies to our new birth.
He created us anew in Christ Jesus for good works "which
God prepared in advance for us to do" (Ephesians 2:10 NIV).
The God who knows everything about us still loves us. With
the psalmist let us declare, "Such knowledge is too wonderful
for me, too lofty for me to attain" (139:6 NIV).

God, how can You know all about everyone who has ever
lived? Your ways are so far beyond my understanding, and
yet You love me. You are so wonderful! Amen.

Every Moment. . .

He will not let your foot slip—
he who watches over you will not slumber.

PSALM 121:3 NIV

The Psalms tell us that God does *not* sleep. He watches over us, never once averting His eyes even for a few quick moments of rest. God guards our every moment. The Lord stays up all night, looking after us as we sleep. He patiently keeps His eyes on us even when we roam. He constantly comforts when fear or illness make us toss and turn. Like a caring parent who tiptoes into a sleeping child's room, God surrounds us even when we don't realize it. We can sleep because God never slumbers.

O God, how grateful I am that You never sleep.
When weariness overtakes me, You guard me like
a mother who watches over her child.
I love You, Father! Amen.

Childlike Faith

Don't let anyone look down on you because you
are young, but set an example for the believers
in speech, in conduct, in love, in faith and in purity.

1 TIMOTHY 4:12 NIV

Much of the wisdom we gain comes through experiences we try to shed in an effort to get back to a purer, more innocent state. Young believers can be a reminder to the older generation of the joy and enthusiasm a pure faith can generate. And they have another important task; after all, "peer pressure" doesn't always have to be negative. The young are best positioned to bring other young folk to God, and that is work fully deserving of respect.

Dear God, help me to rediscover childlike innocence,
the simplicity of faith without doubt. It is in that
purest form of belief that I am nearest to You. Amen.

Joyous Feasts

The Lord said to Moses, "Speak to the Israelites and say to them: 'These are my appointed festivals, the appointed festivals of the Lord, which you are to proclaim as sacred assemblies.'"

LEVITICUS 23:1-2 NIV

During the feast of booths, the Israelites camped out in fragile shelters for seven days as a remembrance of God's care and protection following their escape from Egypt. This joyous feast took place at the end of the harvest season and included a time of thanksgiving to God for the year's crops. Like the Israelites, let's use all our holidays to celebrate God's goodness, reflecting on the blessings He has given us personally and as a nation.

Father, the secular world has excluded You from holidays, especially those set to honor You. As for me, Lord, I will worship You every day, holidays included. Amen.

His Love Endures Forever

God, God, save me! I'm in over my head,
quicksand under me, swamp water over me;
I'm going down for the third time. I'm hoarse
from calling for help, bleary-eyed from
searching the sky for God.

PSALM 69:1–3 MSG

The psalm writers had a very real, genuine relationship with God. They sang praises to God, they got angry with God, they felt abandoned by God, they didn't understand God's slow response. . .and yet they continued to live by faith, deeply convicted that God would overcome. These ancient prayers remind us that nothing can shock God's ears. We can tell Him anything and everything. He won't forsake us—His love endures forever.

O Lord, You know the secrets of my family's hearts.
Teach us to talk to You through every emotion and
every circumstance. Our focus belongs on You.

A Strong Spring

My voice shalt thou hear in the morning, O LORD;
in the morning will I direct my prayer
unto thee, and will look up.
PSALM 5:3 KJV

We need to begin our busy days with a "strong spring," too. Not with just a good cup of coffee, but some time spent with our source of strength. Taking five minutes or an hour—or more if we're really disciplined—in prayer and Bible reading can make the difference in our day. No matter if we're facing wresting kids out of bed or fighting traffic all the way to work, that special time can give us a "spring in our step" today.

Thank You, Lord, for another day. Be my source
of strength today. In Jesus' blessed name, amen.

Renewal of All Things

Then Peter answered and said to Him, "Behold, we have left
everything and followed You; what then will there be for us?"
And Jesus said to them, "You who have followed Me…when
the Son of Man will sit on His glorious throne, you also shall sit
upon twelve thrones, judging the twelve tribes of Israel."
MATTHEW 19:27–28 NASB

None of us will just occupy space in heaven. Our God is
always productive. And this job to which Jesus refers, that
of judging the twelve tribes of Israel, will be given to the
disciples. Have you ever speculated as to what you might
do in heaven? Well, don't worry, it's not going to be anything
like what you've done on earth. Your "boss," after all, will be
perfect. And the tasks you perform will be custom-tailored
to you. "Job satisfaction" will finally fit into our vernacular.

Lord, I can't even imagine what You have in store
for me in heaven. Please keep me faithful to
complete the duties You've called me to on earth.

Hold onto Hope

The prospect of the righteous is joy,
but the hopes of the wicked come to nothing.

PROVERBS 10:28 NIV

Trusting in Jesus gave you new life and hope for eternity. So how do you respond when life becomes dark and dull? Does hope slip away? When no obviously great spiritual works are going on, do not assume God has deserted you. Hold onto Him even more firmly and trust. He will keep His promises. Truly, what other option do you have? Without Him, hope disappears.

Dear heavenly Father, the day I met You was the day
I received life anew. My soul now overflows with hope,
love, peace, and joy. Thank You for saving me!

Everyday Blessings

*But the eyes of the L*ord *are on those who fear him,*
on those whose hope is in his unfailing love.

PSALM 33:18 NIV

The Lord of all creation is watching our every moment and wants to fill us with His joy. He often interrupts our lives with His blessings: butterflies dancing in sunbeams, dew-touched spiderwebs, cotton-candy clouds, and glorious crimson sunsets. The beauty of His creation reassures us of His unfailing love and fills us with hope. But it is up to us to take the time to notice.

May I always be aware of Your lovely creation,
Father God. Your artistry never fails to amaze me!

An End to Mourning

Blessed are those who mourn,
for they will be comforted.
MATTHEW 5:4 NIV

How often do we think of mourning as a good thing? But when it comes to sin, it is. Those who sorrow over their own sinfulness will turn to God for forgiveness. When He willingly responds to their repentance, mourning ends. Comforted by God's pardon, transformed sinners celebrate—and joyous love for Jesus replaces sorrow.

Heavenly Father, thank You for replacing my sorrow
with joy! Your unconditional love floods
my soul. You are good!

Loving Jesus

Looking unto Jesus the author
and finisher of our faith.
HEBREWS 12:2 KJV

God is writing a story of faith through your life. What will it describe? Will it be a chronicle of challenges overcome, like the Old Testament story of Joseph? Or a near tragedy turned into joy, like that of the prodigal son? Whatever your account says, if you love Jesus, the end is never in question. Those who love Him finish in heaven despite their trials on earth. The long, weary path ends in His arms. Today, write a chapter in your faithful narrative of God's love.

God, thank You for helping me write my story.
May my story touch the lives of others and
be a light pointing them to You!

First Love

But you must stay deeply rooted and firm in your faith.
You must not give up the hope you received
when you heard the good news.

COLOSSIANS 1:23 CEV

Do you remember the day you turned your life over to Christ?
Can you recall the flood of joy and hope that coursed through
your veins? Ah, the wonder of first love. Like romantic love that
deepens and broadens with passing years, our relationship
with Jesus evolves into a river of faith that endures the test
of time.

Father, I am so thankful that You are faithful.
Though human relationships may fail,
You are a constant companion
in my life. Thank You!

JOY: Jesus Occupying You

May all who fear you find in me a cause for joy,
for I have put my hope in your word.

PSALM 119:74 NLT

Have you ever met someone you immediately knew was filled with joy? The kind of effervescent joy that bubbles up and overflows, covering everyone around with warmth and love and acceptance. We love to be near people filled with Jesus-joy. And even more, as Christians we want to be like them!

Lord, show me how to radiate Your joy in
the presence of others. I want to be a light for You.

Forever Joy

We don't look at the troubles we can see now. . . .
For the things we see now will soon be gone,
but the things we cannot see will last forever.

2 Corinthians 4:18 nlt

A painter's first brushstrokes look like random blobs—no discernible shape, substance, or clue as to what the completed painting will be. But in time, the skilled artist brings order to perceived chaos. Initial confusion is forgotten in joyful admiration of the finished masterpiece. We often can't see past the blobs of trouble on our life canvases. We must trust that the Artist has a masterpiece underway. And there will be great joy in its completion.

God, You are the Master Artist. I trust You
to create a masterpiece with my life canvas.

A New Day

GOD, treat us kindly. You're our only hope.
First thing in the morning, be there for us!
When things go bad, help us out!

ISAIAH 33:2 MSG

Every day is a new day, a new beginning, a new chance to enjoy our lives—each day is a new day with God. We can focus on the things that matter most: worshipping Him, listening to Him, and being in His presence. No matter what happened the day before, we have a fresh start to enjoy a deeper relationship with Him: a fresh canvas every twenty-four hours.

Before I get out of bed in the morning, let me say these
words and mean them: "The LORD has done it this very day;
let us rejoice today and be glad" (Psalm 118:24 NIV).

Scripture Index